Lay Workers for Christ

Lay Workers
for Christ

edited by Reverend George L. Kane

with an introduction by
Valerian Cardinal Gracias
Archbishop of Bombay

57-1090

THE NEWMAN PRESS
WESTMINSTER, MARYLAND
1957

Nihil obstat: EDWARD A. CERNY, S. S., D. D.
　　　　　　　Censor Librorum

Imprimatur: MOST REVEREND FRANCIS P. KEOUGH, D. D.
　　　　　　　Archbishop of Baltimore

June 4, 1957

The *nihil obstat* and *imprimatur* are official declarations that a book or
pamphlet is free of doctrinal and moral error. No implication is contained
therein that those who have granted the *nihil obstat* and *imprimatur* agree
with the opinions expressed.

Copyright © 1957 by THE NEWMAN PRESS
Library of Congress Catalog Card Number: 57–11817
Printed in the United States of America

Acknowledgments

The editor wishes to acknowledge with thanks permission to re-
print copyrighted material as follows: "Making a Convert" by
Floyd Anderson, reprinted from *Our Sunday Visitor,* July 22,
1956. "Why My Children Go to Catholic Schools" by Dennis Day,
reprinted from *The Catholic Digest,* August, 1956. "Apostolate to
the Worker," condensed from *The Long Loneliness* by Dorothy
Day, copyright by Harper & Brothers, New York, 1952. "Money
and Us," by Margaret Thompson, reprinted from *Information,*
September, 1956.

920
K13L

to
the laity in the Church
in the hope
that it may inspire many
to dynamic zeal in the apostolate

this book
is affectionately dedicated
by the editor

Preface

Even a superficial reading of the history of the Church will reveal how effectively she has taught and applied the doctrines of faith revealed by Christ. Every age presents its special problems, and for every problem the Church of Christ has a solution. It matters not what form the solution takes—the establishment of a religious congregation to undertake a specific work, the election of an illustrious pontiff destined to meet a particular crisis, the timely canonization of a great saint to inspire the faithful, a re-emphasis and a special application of one of her doctrines—the Church in one way or another meets the challenge of every century, thereby displaying her perennial youth and her supernatural wisdom.

Thus in our day when the new paganism attacks the very foundations of Christianity and the new atheism denies the dignity of man, the Church stresses the glorious doctrine of the Mystical Body of Christ. And to counteract the menace of secularism that would divorce religion from life and separate God from the world He created, the Church calls for a zealous and dynamic lay apostolate in which all lay members of the Mystical Body who have even a limited measure of talent and opportunity are invited, nay urged, to share actively in the redemptive work of Christ. In this the Church is not experimenting; rather is she reverting to the earliest Christian traditions. If the pagans during the first centuries of the Church were impressed with the intensity of Christian charity, they were also impelled to marvel at the zeal of lay Christians for the spread of their Faith. Yes, the lay apostolate, like the doctrine of the Mystical Body, is as old as the Church itself, but in our day it has been brought into new focus by the exigencies of the times and the almost universal shortage of priests.

In his address to the World Congress of Lay Apostles held in Rome in 1951, Pope Pius XII pointed out:

> We cannot . . . say that all are called in an equal measure to the apostolate, if we understand that word in its strictest sense. For God has not given to all the opportunity and the necessary ability for such an undertaking.

But those possessing the ability and the opportunity are called to active work in the apostolate. Thus the Holy Father in the same address states:

> The lay apostolate, in the strict sense, is undoubtedly part and parcel of Catholic Action and takes the form of different societies and groups approved by the Church for specific apostolic work. But it is at the same time wider in extent than that; it claims as apostles all those men and women who, in an effort to bring men to the truth and to the life of grace, seize upon every opportunity to do good by whatever means present themselves.

In spite of the presence and activity of zealous lay apostles in greater or smaller number in every age of the Church's history, the recent emphasis on the lay apostolate is somewhat surprising and even startling to many of the laity themselves. The truth that they have a unique, individual, indispensable and urgent role to play in the life and work of the Church comes as a momentous and thrilling discovery. It satisfies a deep yearning in the Catholic heart; it presents the noblest kind of challenge; it offers the opportunity to share in the most sublime mission on earth. In one person this discovery evokes the response of a total, dedicated service to Christ's cause; it induces another to add to his regular occupation some special form of the apostolate—spending himself and being spent for Christ in every leisure moment; still another makes his profession or business or work his particular apostolate, thus elevating it to a new and supernaturalized level—himself a witness to Christ in the world through the irrefutable testimony of an exemplary Catholic life. Each is an apostle in greater or less degree, according to his opportunities and circumstances.

The present anthology represents an attempt to present various forms of the apostolate through the interesting and attractive medium of autobiography. As Cardinal Gracias suggests, the earlier volumes in this series, WHY I BECAME A PRIEST, WHY I ENTERED THE CONVENT, and WHY I BECAME A BROTHER, were necessarily addressed to a limited number of our youth, but LAY WORKERS FOR CHRIST is addressed to all.

It is understandable that many of the authors of this book were hesitant, even reluctant, to write about themselves and their work for God and for souls. But conscious of Christ's directive, they consented to let their light shine before men in the hope that others might be guided along the same or similar paths.

It remains only for the editor to express his gratitude to His Eminence, Cardinal Gracias, for writing the Introduction, and to the several contributors for their chapters. May the book inspire many of our youth to dedicate themselves, as totally as their natural endowments and circumstances of life permit, to the service of Christ as lay apostles.

GEORGE L. KANE [1]

North Sydney, N. S.
March 22, 1957

---

[1] Reverend George L. Kane is Director of Religious Education and Vocations in the Diocese of Antigonish, Nova Scotia.

Contents

Introduction

HIS EMINENCE, VALERIAN CARDINAL GRACIAS

Archbishop of Bombay

T HE articles which make up the contents of *Lay Workers for Christ* have, in their number and variety, both an illustrative and a representative character. They serve to indicate and illustrate in some detail the various fields of the Church's apostolate to which laymen are devoting their gifts and the wealth of their accumulated experience. In the selection of writers, the editor, it would seem, has aimed at some degree of representation so that the contributors may stand out, not without merit, among the ever-increasing army of men and women playing their role today in their own restricted spheres in the furtherance of the lay apostolate. While the appeal of the three previous volumes of vocational autobiographies edited by Father Kane is necessarily to a comparatively small minority, the present volume should, in one sense, be the most valuable in the entire series in that it will open up avenues of worthwhile, apostolic activity to all our young people. In its pages they will have inspirational reading matter that may serve to direct their energies and focus their ideals in the direction of God, the Church and souls.

Unhesitatingly and gladly have I accepted the invitation to write this Introduction, not only because of the special attention given nowadays to the lay apostolate, but also because of my intimate association from my early ministry with the efforts of laymen in the field of Catholic Action, especially in India. My great interest in this field has increased even more in recent years by the inspiration I have received from the World Assemblies and National Congresses in which I have had the good fortune to participate: the World Congress of the Lay Apostolate held in Rome in 1951; the University Students' Congress of Madras, India, in 1952; The First Asian Meeting of the Lay Apostolate in Manila, Philippines, in 1955; and the Lay Leaders' Conference of Nagpur, India, in 1955. At all these meetings one could not but be edified and heartened by the keen awareness on the part of the delegates of the dangers confronting the Church, their realization of the glorious opportunities for service and heroism, their insistent demand for the training of such lay leaders as would show, in the words of St. Paul to Titus, "an example of good works in doctrine, in integrity."

Successive Popes have made many important pronouncements on various aspects of the lay apostolate. The following extracts from the discourse of the Holy Father at the conclusion of the World Congress of 1951 ought to merit the special attention of every lay worker:

The expression—*"emancipation of the laity"*—which is heard here and there is hardly pleasing to Us. In the Kingdom of grace all are regarded as adults. The appeal for the help of the laity is not due to the failure or frustration of the clergy in the face of its present task. The layman is called to the apostolate *as the collaborator of the priest* . . . because of the penury of clergy . . .

When we compare the Lay Apostolate, or more precisely the layman of Catholic Action, to *an instrument in the hands of the hierarchy,* according to the expression which has become current, we understand the comparison in this sense: namely, that the ecclesiastical superiors use him in a manner in which the Creator and Lord uses rational creatures as instruments, as second causes, *"disposing of them with great favor."* (Wisdom XII:18.)

These observations of the Holy Father indicate very clearly what the position of the layman is in the scheme of the apostolate of the Church; how valuable is his collaboration, how eagerly it is, and ought to be, sought by the hierarchy; and how necessary it is for the conviction to grow that the lay apostolate is an urgent necessity of the times. For the lay apostolate is not a luxury of devotion or a work of supereroga- tion. It is rather a plain duty which lies upon each of us according to his abilities. The rich genius of the Church has produced different forms of the lay apostolate to suit the needs of the times and the various needs of the people. Though the layman is no new phenomenon in the Church, and is as old as the Church in his vocation and activity, as history bears out, it is however in the exigent circumstances of the Church today and the world in which she is situated that the active collabo- ration of the laity in her apostolic work is of prime importance. The vast growth of population, the expansion of Christianity all over the world, the insufficiency of priests and nuns, the growing anti-Christian and anticlerical spirit of the age, the growth of large-scale industries, of the predominance of the economic motive, and many other factors have created cir- cumstances which call for the active collaboration of the laity in the apostolate of the hierarchy.

A deeper and fuller understanding of the Christian voca- tion must necessarily constitute one of the doctrinal founda- tions of the lay apostolate. The revival of the doctrine of the Mystical Body of Christ has greatly helped to correct an inadequate concept of the Christian vocation, by leading us to a deeper level of understanding of the function of the Church. Hence, the more we understand what the Church is in her- self, the sounder the grasp we have of the spirit which binds her external communicants into a living fold, the clearer will be the concept of the Christian vocation and its effect on our daily life, *both individually and in society*. I say advisedly, "individually and in society," because the Christian cannot sanctify himself, much less sanctify others, by a mystical escape from the social order. All the social values of mankind ought to enter, like individual values, into the Christian life. Hence it is that, in so many papal documents, we note the appeal made insistently for the wide diffusion of principles of the Faith in their application in private, domestic, and civil life.

The individual and society are two facets of one and the same
perfection. As Dr. Karl Adam has put it so well: "Catholicism
is the affirmation of values along the whole line, the most
comprehensive and the noblest accessibility to all good, a union
of nature with grace, of art with religion, of knowledge with
faith . . . so that God may be all in all."

We must not put the cart before the horse. If the presence
of the Christian in the world is to act as the leaven in the
dough, the light in the darkness, and the salt of the earth, the
action of the leaven must be strong, the light must shine; the
salt that has lost its savour is worthless. Therefore, "give the
very first place to the formation of the interior spirit, without
which all exterior action is futile and must be looked upon
with suspicion." (Pius XII, *Letter to Marian Sodalities,* April
15, 1950.)

I bless the efforts of the editor in producing this volume and
all the distinguished contributors for their valuable studies.
May the youth of the world profit by the learning and zeal
with which the writers have made their contributions.

Lay Workers for Christ

Love's Dream Fulfilled

CATHERINE DE HUECK DOHERTY [1]

T HERE was no denying it! I had found my vocation!

But it appeared so strange to me, so utterly impossible, that I laid it away, as people do beautiful, fragile garments, within the depths of my heart. I was sure that all I could do with it was to take it out from time to time and wonder how a human being could get the idea that this beautiful, precious vocation might be hers.

There was no way that I could see, at the time, of embracing this "strange vocation," and yet I continued to take it out more often from the depths of my heart, and consider it from all its beautiful angles. It seemed to grow on me, too—as a dream grows in the night. Only this was a dream dreamt in God!

[1] Catherine (Mrs. Eddie) Doherty, the former Baroness de Hueck, was born in Russia, where she belonged to the wealthy class of the nobility. Reduced to poverty and forced to flee the country as a result of the Communist Revolution, she came to Canada. In various occupations—as factory worker, waitress, laundress, sales clerk and maid—she came into close contact with the poor and yearned to devote her life to serving them. Her particular apostolate took the form of Friendship Houses, which she established in several centers in Canada and the United States. In 1951, Mrs. Doherty had the privilege of a private audience with the Holy Father, who suggested that she consider forming her group of lay workers into a Secular Institute. The members of the Canadian branch, at Madonna House, Combermere, Ontario, where Mrs. Doherty and her husband reside, voted to take the necessary steps toward this objective, and formal application has been made to the Holy See. The official name of this Secular Institute, already approved by the diocesan authorities is *Domus Dominae,* House of Our Lady, i.e., Madonna House.

In 1926–27, when this "vocation" entered my heart, this
dream became the reality of my soul. No one had ever heard
of anything like it before. I know. I talked to ninety-nine
priests, by my own careful count. And every one of them,
smiling indulgently, pointed out to me that it was nothing but
a passing fancy, a dream without a substance . . . for my
true vocation was both palpable and visible, and bore the name
of George, who was my son, aged six or seven at the time.
Since I had lost my husband, the good priests went on to say,
I had a double duty toward my son. I must be father, mother,
breadwinner, friend, counsellor.

I knew that they were right. My holy religion told me that.
Yet here I was, asking one priest after another. I could not
give up that dream dreamt in God, that fragile, unreal thing
of beauty that filled my heart and soul with hunger and fire.

Yet when you come to think of it, "my vocation" was
simplicity itself. I wanted to sell what I possessed, give it to
the poor (literally and personally as it said in the Gospel about
the rich young man), take up my cross, and follow Christ into
the slums of our big cities and the hidden, substandard rural
areas.

I wanted to serve these poor personally, be poor with them,
and witness to Christ before them by a life lived in Gospel-like
simplicity, in the spirit of the counsels of perfection, with or
without simple private vows. *And I wanted to do it as a lay
person . . . not as a member of a religious order. . . .*

Why? Because I who had been very rich once, and a member of the upper classes in Russia, had been forcibly shown by
God that riches and power and social position are in truth
vanity and nothing but vanity; for in three days, because of
the Communist Revolution, I was reduced from the top of the
human heap to a hungry, cold, penniless, destitute fugitive,
hiding for my life.

God spared me. I managed to escape and make my way
with my husband, the Baron de Hueck, to Canada. There my
son George was born, two months after my arrival. Then
followed years of poverty and hardship. The Baron, who had

been shell-shocked and gassed in World War One, was ailing.
. . . I had to be the breadwinner.

Factory worker . . . waitress . . . laundress . . . sales clerk
. . maid . . . I was all of these . . . and learned much in
each capacity. I learned, above all, that in the richest continent
of the world, communism was fast coming in amongst the
masses. I learned that one could be hungry in the middle of
Fifth Avenue, that one could be utterly lonely and desolate on
the corner of Broadway and 42nd Street.

I learned more. I learned that Christ, and He crucified, was
virtually a stranger to America's masses, especially to those
that no one had time to bother about.

Sharing their life of drab poverty, strange and lonely myself,
I felt what they felt. I wept with them. Once in a while I
laughed with them.

Eventually, due to my good education and some fortunate
circumstances, I left the slum areas. But they never left me.
They had imprinted themselves on my very soul . . . my
very heart. They were like a burning seal.

So when I lost my husband, my thoughts went back to
them. This time *I wanted to go to the slums to share that
life as the servant of the poor; for the love of Christ who was
in their midst . . . and for the sheer simple love of each of
them.* . . .

But, as the good ninety-nine priests so clearly showed me,
my vocation was still right in front of me. My little son!

What is a woman to do when her desire to serve the Desired
One in this particular way burns night and day in her soul?
It did in mine. And it seemed at times that in truth it was a
terrible thing to fall into the hands of the living God! Then
again I found myself in some strange depths, wondering if I
was not a prey to illusions. Perhaps even the Prince of Darkness was working his wiles on me!

It is not easy even to try to describe this strange and long
fight of mine. The sleepless nights . . . the long endless days
. . . the praying . . . the inability to pray any more . . . the
seeking of advice . . . the knocking at priests' doors . . . the
certainty of the words of advice . . . and the burning hunger

that would not allow me to rest! Where are the words that would express all this?

Finally I went to my Ordinary, the late Archbishop Neil McNeil of Toronto. I had learned at my mother's knee that the Bishop of one's diocese is one's spiritual father, that he possesses the fulness of the priesthood, and that his decisions are in truth God's decisions.

The good prelate listened to my outpourings—for to him I opened my soul utterly. He listened for some forty minutes in silence. When I had finished, he looked at me sorrowfully, yet withal joyously (or so it seemed to me). And he said, "Child, God has given you a vocation fifty years ahead of your times!"

He allowed me—after making me wait a year to be sure, and also after obtaining the consent of my son—he allowed me to do what I desired! My joy had no end. My heart was filled with an endless alleluia!

I found out that it takes time to sell what one possesses. And during this time the few friends in whom I had confided, with whom I had shared my joy, came and asked to join me! Two young men and three young women.

Terrified, for I had not thought of a group, merely of a "lonely apostolate," I hurried to the Archbishop and told him of this new development. He suggested that God had evidently given me an additional cross, that of being a foundress, that I should accept it, and the five lay followers, and seek a living via begging and praying. I obeyed. Thus the first Friendship House Lay Apostolic group was born on October 15, 1930.

The deepening of a spiritual life . . . through daily Mass, Prime, spiritual reading, Compline, the rosary . . . short days of recollection . . . little retreats . . . Poverty . . . Chastity . . . Obedience . . . lived in the fulness of their spirit. Such was our first "Little Constitution."

Yet even then, from the very start, we had understood—that first things must come first, and that—*to be before God came before the doing for God*. And that that *being*, as well as that *doing*, required constantly expanding our knowledge of God. For knowledge led to ever greater love. *And fundamentally*

our apostolate to the market places and to the masses . . .
was the apostolate . . . "to love!"

The group grew. Other Ordinaries invited us. (We came only by such official invitations.) A Friendship House opened in Ottawa, another in Hamilton. We crossed the border. Friendship House, Harlem, New York, was born in 1938, then the Chicago Friendship House was opened. Marathon, Wisconsin, came next. Then Washington, D.C., followed by Portland, Oregon, and Shreveport, Louisiana. Some closed, for various reasons; others opened.

From 1930 to 1938 we worked with labor, children, and information centres in Canada. In the United States the work was devoted to interracial justice, exclusively with Negroes. In 1947 I recrossed into Canada, coming to Madonna House, Combermere, Ontario, at the invitation of Bishop W. J. Smith of Pembroke, to work in the rural apostolate. A second house was opened in Edmonton, Alberta, working with Skid Row folks; and another in Whitehorse, Yukon Territory, the cold, Arctic region where we became co-missionaries (always lay) of the Oblates of Mary Immaculate, working with pagan Indians and with all the needs of a frontier town.

Up to 1951 Madonna House was still the Canadian Province of Friendship House. But during my visit to Rome, on the occasion of the First Lay Congress I had the privilege of a private audience with the Holy Father and heard him speak of consecrated dedicated groups (Secular Institutes). I realized that His Holiness greatly desired such Institutes, and I brought the message back to the American and Canadian groups.

The Canadian group immediately voted to take the needed steps to become a Secular Institute. The workers in the United States did not feel this was for them.

Now we here in Canada call ourselves *Madonna House (Domus Dominae) and have become a diocesan secular institute* awaiting final approval of the Holy See, whereas our brothers and sisters below the border remain a more loosely-knit Catholic Action group under the name of Friendship House.

Broad is the concept of the lay apostolate of Catholic Action.

And all are welcome, said His Holiness, to labor in it. To me the slow evolution in the depth of my strange new-old vocation seems wonderful. It began so simply. So directly. A little stream. It grew. It flowed into the bigger streams of the Church. And now it has come to rest within her heart!

It seems incredible that we have become part and parcel of its inner family. It also seems incredible that, bound by the three vows (yes, Eddie, my second husband, and I both took the vows, including that of Chastity—it is so little to give when God asks!), we still remain *lay*.

Secular Institutes, though their members are in a state of canonical perfection, *are still lay,* not religious.

Otherwise our Constitutions have changed but little. They still have the same foundations of long and arduous spiritual, academic, practical training for the great apostolate of the market place. We still place the prayer life ahead of the life of action—*to be before God, then do for God.*

We still enter a diocese only on the *mandate of its Ordinary.* We still have chaplains, only now they are our own. For our Institute is composed of priests, lay men, and lay women—something like the Opus Dei.

Strange, you will say, this saga of a dream dreamt in God . . . of fragile beauty laid deep in a bewildered, hungry, burning heart . . . to be taken out again and again! Yes . . . perhaps . . . But the impossible takes only a second longer for God. . . .

And I thank Him, if a human being can so thank the Creator, for having allowed me in on the ground floor, in the pioneering of this form of the lay apostolate. The pioneering is done. Now it is coming into its own. Now many understand the glorious call of God to men . . . the call to witness to Christ in the market places of the world! Alleluia! Alleluia!

If you too feel the call of this adventure with God, be not afraid. He will walk with you all the way. . . . And His Mother will walk with you too, and teach you the ways of the lay apostolate—for wasn't she a *lay* woman, par excellence? And isn't this the Marian Age—the Age of the Lay Apostolate too?

Why My Children Go to Catholic Schools

DENNIS DAY [1]

as told to Charles Oxton

In 1939, it was an even longer jump from a college campus to a major broadcasting studio than it is today. I made it "with the help of God and two sober policemen," as my County Mayo-born mother used to say, on almost my first try. I made it because of her prayers and the prayers of my father, sister, brothers, and relatives and friends in and around the Bronx, where I was born.

But I made it for another reason too: the influence of my training in Catholic schools.

It happened like this. Jack Benny had let it be known that he was in the market for a tenor to replace his featured soloist, Kenny Baker, who had announced his intention to launch out on his own. I was fresh out of Manhattan College, where I had been president of the glee club.

I found myself on the horns of a dilemma. I wanted to make singing a career. I also wanted to repay my parents for their struggle to give me a good Catholic education, and I wasn't quite sure I could do it with my voice alone. My total professional experience consisted of a few guest appearances

---

[1] Dennis Day, the popular and beloved tenor of radio and television, was born Owen Patrick McNulty in the Bronx, New York. He had planned to study law, but his talent in music led to a radio contract with the Jack Benny show and success in Hollywood. Mr. Day attributes much of that success to his training in Catholic schools, and insists on the same type of education for his children.

with Larry Clinton's orchestra and several sustaining sessions over one of the local radio stations, WHN.

With the country just getting over the worst depression in our history, and Europe on the brink of war, it hardly seemed the time to go tilting at musical windmills, and yet I felt that I had to give it a try. If I didn't make it, and pretty fast, I was determined to enroll at Fordham University Law School and use my Gaelic gift of gab (with a monicker like Owen Patrick McNulty, my real name, how could I miss?) to impress clients and influence juries instead. Luckily for me, and perhaps for the legal profession, the Benny-Baker split-up pried open the door of opportunity.

The day I went down to the NBC studios, there were half a dozen other young hopefuls trying out for the job. All of them had followed the same procedure I had. They had made recordings in advance and submitted them to Mary Livingstone—Mrs. Benny, in private life—for a hearing. On the basis of those recordings, they had been called down to do their stuff for Jack on the spot.

Exactly how long it took before my turn came around, I don't know. But I do know it was plain torture sitting there, listening to the others audition and wondering if I would do as well. Looking back now, I'm sure the others were as nervous as I was, but they managed to cover it up better, by wisecracking and pretending it was all in the day's work. As each one's name was called over the intercom from the control room, he would answer with a nonchalant "Yeah" or "Okay," and then saunter confidently up to the mike.

I had half made up my mind to copy them, to show my professional *savoir-faire,* when Jack's voice came booming at me, calling my stage name, Dennis Day.

Forgetting my resolution, I answered instinctively, "Yes, please?" just as I'd been taught to do in school whenever I was called on to recite. Maybe students in other schools are taught to answer the same way, as a mark of respect toward their elders, but I'm sure none of them are trained to the extent that Catholic students are. Respect for those who are older or who are in authority over them starts the first day in kindergarten and continues until they get their college degrees. Without getting too profound (and who expects a tenor to get profound?), I may say that the whole concept of showing respect for age and authority stems from a consciousness of our relationship to God. He is the source of all power and authority, and by showing respect to our elders we honor Him.

Anyway, those two words, "Yes, please?" propelled me to Hollywood on the wings of a contract to appear regularly on the Benny program.

Just before I left to join the Navy during the Second World War, when Jack was bidding me good-by, he explained how he'd come to hire me over everyone else. "I'd listened to your records and had a pretty good idea of what you could do," he told me. "That little bit of politeness clinched it. In this business, courtesy and respect are so rare that you can't help but sit up and take notice when you encounter them. The moment I heard you answer 'yes, please?' that day in the studio, I told Mary you were the one for the job."

I am sending each of my six children to Catholic schools. My two oldest, Patrick, seven, and Dennis, six, are already in parochial school; a third, Michael, five, starts kindergarten this September. My six youngsters—and whatever other children God may bless us with—will get a *thorough* Catholic education, right up to the time they finish college and strike out on their own.

I will send my children to Catholic schools for three reasons: 1. because it is my duty as a Catholic parent to do so; 2. because a Catholic education is the best form of "insurance" to safeguard their spiritual future; 3. because only a Catholic education will give them a complete education, in mind, body, and soul.

There is nothing startlingly new about all this. Others have stated it much better. And I'm not doing anything extraordinary. On the contrary, with the earth half free and half slave, with decency and morality only catchwords for far too many people, I would be criminally negligent if I failed to give my kids the start in life they need.

My mother's joke about my success being due to the "help

of God and two sober policemen" has more truth in it than whimsey. A Catholic education and the Catholic Church, she used to tell me, constitute the two "policemen" who make it possible to keep on the road to heaven. I would deprive my children of the aid of one of these two policemen if I did not send them to Catholic schools.

It's true that giving Patrick, Dennis, Michael, Margaret, Eileen, and baby Paul a Catholic education presents no financial problem for me at present. Many of you are probably saying, "It's all very well for him to talk. He doesn't have to worry about money for tuition and books and clothes."

I can only answer that I would still think the way I do if the ball should bounce the wrong way (and in this business there is no guarantee it won't) and I should have to pinch and scrape to make ends meet.

I wasn't born with a silver spoon in my mouth. Our neighborhood in the Bronx, while it wasn't the worst in the area, by any means, did have its shadowy side. It had its quota of hoodlums and teen-age gangs and basement hangouts, and left to my own devices, without the steadying influence of a good Catholic home and a good Catholic education, I would have got into plenty of trouble.

Thanks to my parents, I wasn't left to my own devices. They saw to it that I got understanding and discipline and moral training every day at home. And they made sure I got the same treatment in the classroom.

It wasn't easy. My father, a stationary engineer, never made more than $60 a week, and yet, somehow, he and my mother managed not only to give me and my sister and my four brothers the necessities of life but they also provided us with a thoroughly Catholic education, right up to and through college.

How they did it, I don't know. I admit that the cost of living wasn't so high in those days as it is today. Still, supporting a home and putting six children through college on a salary of $60 a week was a pretty good trick, no matter how you look at it. I often wonder if I would have been able to do the same.

When I was nine or ten and had a paper route for the

Bronx *Home News,* I used to think that maybe I would quit school and go to work as soon as I was able to get my working papers. Young as I was, I knew that anything my brothers or I could do to swell the family income would take that much pressure off my father and mother and make things better all around.

I didn't entertain the notion very long. The first time I even hinted at what was in my mind, I was told to forget it. I was made to understand that my job was to develop my brain and save my soul. If any of us wished to help out by working after school, that was all right. But one way or another we were going to stay in a Catholic school.

In 1930, after being graduated from St. Benedict's, our parish school, I was enrolled at Cathedral High uptown. By then, my brother John (now my business manager), was at the Catholic University of America in Washington, D.C., with intentions of becoming a lay Brother. My brother Frank was at LaSalle Academy in the heart of the lower New York East Side. Jim, now a doctor married to movie star Ann Blyth; Billy, at present a captain in the Army Medical corps; and my sister Margaret were all still in elementary grades.

At Cathedral, I set no worlds afire scholastically, but I did manage to hold my own. The one thing that helped me to do as well as I did was the spiritual atmosphere that surrounded all my activities. At home, the Morning Offering, grace before and after meals, and night prayers were such a part of family routine that we would no more have thought of skipping any one of them than we would have thought of missing Sunday Mass. On evenings when we were all together, we said the family rosary. If a baseball game between the Giants and the Dodgers was being broadcast over the radio at the same time —well, we missed it, that was all.

At school, the situation was pretty much the same without, of course, the give-and-take of family life. We were made to toe the line in our studies. But we were also made to understand that even if our scholastic achievements bordered on genius and we lost sight of our eternal destiny, we would have failed. I remember one teacher telling us, "Save your soul, and you'll be richer than Rockefeller. Lose it, and all the money in the world won't buy your way out of hell."

In 1934, I entered Manhattan College with my mind half made up to become a lawyer unless my new-found love for music promised greater rewards. I still worked after school at odd jobs around the neighborhood; my brothers did the same. In my senior year at Manhattan, I was elected president of the glee club and attracted sufficient attention to prompt Larry Clinton to ask me to make guest appearances with his band.

Shortly after graduation, the incident with Jack Benny took place, and I gave up thinking of legal briefs to toil in the California sun. In 1944, I entered the Navy as an ensign (an emergency operation for appendicitis delayed my enlistment almost a year). I was discharged on St. Patrick's day in 1946, as a lieutenant, junior grade. In 1947, I met my wife, Margaret Ellen Almquist, of Southgate, a Los Angeles suburb. In January, 1948, we were married at Mission San Juan Capistrano, and a year later we welcomed our first son, Patrick.

Like all fathers who served, I am constantly besieged with demands from my offspring to tell them of my exploits during the Second World War. Naturally, I try not to destroy their picture of me as a combination Hopalong Cassidy-Gene Autry-Flash Gordon. I did serve as a line officer with the amphibious forces before being ordered to head a special service unit to tour the Pacific area. While my experiences will never go down in naval history, they do seem to make passably good listening, at least for youthful McNulty ears.

I tell them of life aboard a fighting ship; of the spine-tingling sensation that accompanies every call to battle stations; of beach landings and the thundering barrage of heavy guns; of the time a Japanese suicide plane crashed into the side of an aircraft carrier when we were putting on a show for the officers and men, and killed 27 of the crew.

But I tell them of other things, too. I tell them of men saying their rosaries while standing watch in gun turrets; of chaplains and sailors reciting the prayers for the dying in the darkness of the Pacific night; of the time I served midnight Mass celebrated at Pearl Harbor on Christmas eve, 1944, for a congregation of servicemen from every branch of the armed forces.

And when my children are old enough to understand fully, I'll tell them that I never came across a man with a really solid Catholic education and background who ever got into serious trouble. There must have been a few bad apples, I suppose, but I never ran into one of them.

Watching my kids now as they romp around the living room in the evening, I try to picture them as they will be ten, fifteen, or twenty years hence. Will they be upright, God-fearing men and women, a credit to their Church and to their country? They will be as long as I have anything to say about it!

Campaigner for Christ

DAVID GOLDSTEIN [1]

OVER fifty years in the Catholic Church! Over fifty years of battle for truth against error! Over fifty years of religious and moral certitude that have been a joy! That is the story I am to unfold.

It is a commonplace to say that people are very much interested in other people, sometimes as a study of human nature through human experiences and, then again, through mere inquisitiveness. Therefore, it is not a surprise to find the question most often presented to me to be "What caused your conversion?" It is the one question I always hesitate to answer, though not merely because it is of a personal nature, a question that pries into the very soul of one's being. It is because

[1] David Goldstein was born in London, England, of Netherland Jewish parents, who emigrated to the United States when he was about one year old. The family first settled in New York but several years later moved to Boston. There Dr. Goldstein, eager to better the lot of the laboring classes, became an active member of the Socialist Party. His interest in social problems caused him to study the teaching of the Catholic Church on marriage, capital and labor, and other questions. His search for truth led to his baptism in Immaculate Conception Church, Boston, on May 21, 1905.

While a socialist Dr. Goldstein imbibed a propaganda spirit which he has never lost and which he has used most effectively in spreading Catholic truth. In collaboration with another convert, Mrs. Martha Moore Avery, he founded in Boston in 1916 the Catholic Truth Guild, whose name was later changed to Catholic Campaigners for Christ. For forty-five years, he has been engaged in bringing Catholic truth to the man in the street. On the public platform, in lecture halls, on street corners—wherever he could find an audience—Dr. Goldstein has spent himself in spreading the good tidings of the Church founded by Christ. Among his nine books are *Campaigners for Christ Hand-*

DAVID GOLDSTEIN 17

years of introspection and daily reception of the Bread of Angels deepen the realization that the part God plays in conversion to the Catholic Church is so great that the incidents along the journey are, at best, only of secondary importance, interesting though they be to those who hear them.

The instruments strewed along my journey from Marx to Christ must be noted in order to tell the story of my conversion. To understand properly what I am about to relate, it is necessary to say that my road to the Catholic Church was by way of socialism, hence my conversion was from Marx to Christ rather than from the Synagogue to Christ.

Looking back, I can see, as do all converts, that my vision of the Catholic Church was greatly beclouded, because of obstacles in my mind and heart of a hostile nature. My misconceptions and prejudices were, some of them, so deeply ingrained (as they are in Jews) that they may be said to be inherited. They were obstacles that had to be overcome before it was possible to look at the Catholic Church with the intention of seeing her as she claims to be, as she is, the one Christ-made institution in the world. After all, we must be friendly toward an institution, as we must be toward a person, to evaluate an institution or a person correctly, for God rarely strikes us from our horse, as He did Saul of Tarsus. It was during my fight against the socialist concept of the family that, by God's grace, the first obstacle was removed, that of indif-

book, *What Say You?* (a quiz book), *Autobiography of a Campaigner for Christ*, and *Letters of a Hebrew Catholic to Mr. Isaacs.* Today, at the age of eighty-seven, he continues to write his weekly column in the Boston *Pilot*.

On April 3, 1955, following a Solemn Pontifical Mass at St. Clement's Eucharistic Shrine in Boston, a testimonial dinner was given at the Hotel Somerset in commemoration of the approaching fiftieth anniversary of Dr. Goldstein's baptism. On that occasion Archbishop Cushing presented him with the papal documents designating him a Knight of St. Gregory the Great, and said in part:

"His life as a pioneer lay apostle serves to show what a great opportunity is open to informed and loyal Catholic laymen and laywomen to spread the truth about the Church, by word as well as by example. . . . It is true that the name of David Goldstein is known through the length and breadth of the land, but it is known only incidentally to the divine cause to which he has given himself with fulness and dedication."

ference toward what the Catholic Church teaches. It was the
obstacle that had to be removed before an interest in her
doctrine could be awakened.

So favorably was I impressed with the principle of the
indissolubility of the marriage bond, to which the Catholic
Church has adhered throughout the Christian ages, that I
upheld it against the socialist concept of freedom to sunder
unions at will. I was conscious of the fact that this was the
point at which I had become friendly toward the Catholic
Church, though I would simply have laughed at any suggestion that it meant I would some day accept all of her teachings.

This incident was followed by a study of the position of the
Catholic Church toward socialism, for I always knew she
was opposed to it. Moreover, I was in the proper studious
frame of mind to appreciate arguments against socialism.
Hence, I put my whole being, so to speak, into the study of the
Encyclical, *Rerum Novarum,* by Pope Leo XIII, the like of
which I had never before seen. It became my vade mecum in
the battle I waged against socialism. In the meetings my group
of anti-socialists held on Boston Common, in 1903, immediately after my resignation from the socialist movement,
the positive arguments in that great document were used
against socialism.

Association with Martha Moore Avery and acquaintance
with her daughter, Katharine, played a vital part in my
journey from Marx to Christ; hence, it is necessary to say a
word about their relation to my conversion. Mrs. Avery and I
were interested in the same intellectual issues, especially those
of a sociological character. We complemented each other in
our work: She was a master in getting at the basic principle
involved in any issue, no matter how profound or vague it
might be, often taking a pencil or piece of chalk to diagram
the principle. My forte was data. While rarely memorizing
anything, I was able instantly to recall, somewhat in detail,
whatever I saw in newspapers, magazines and books. So our
intellectual association was a joy to both of us, of which
neither of us ever tired. It was but natural that religion should

come up in our conversations, though the Catholic Church did not enter into consideration until the time we fought against the socialist concept of the family.

An incident in Montreal played an interesting part in moving Martha Moore Avery toward the Catholic Church. Being entertained by a Catholic family, while lecturing in that city, she noted the exquisite manners of the daughters of her hostess. It caused her to inquire, "Where did your daughters get their fine breeding?" The mother replied that it came largely from their convent school training, from years of association with Catholic Sisters, whose lives are devoted to the cultivation of the moral and intellectual character of students in their institutions of learning.

This made a deep impression upon Mrs. Avery. So, when her daughter, Katharine, graduated, in 1899, from one of the leading high schools in Boston, she went to La Prairie, Province of Quebec, to a school conducted by the Sisters of the Congregation de Notre Dame, an order of nuns founded in Montreal by Blessed Marguerite Bourgeoys about three hundred years ago. There Katharine was to receive some of the admirable French culture that the Sisters in that great Canadian order expertly impart to their students.

Not long afterwards—on Friday, March 9, 1900, she was baptised by Reverend Martin Callaghan, in St. Patrick's Church, Montreal, with the full consent of her mother. A few years later Katharine Avery became Sister St. Mary Martha, C.N.D.

This conversion intensified Martha Moore Avery's interest in the Catholic Church, in which she herself was baptised by Reverend Denis T. O'Sullivan, S.J., in the Immaculate Conception Church, Boston, on May 1, 1903, slightly more than than three years after the baptism of her daughter.

The conversion of Katharine Avery into Sister St. Mary Martha, the discussion of religion with Martha Moore Avery, which was more and more encouraged by the beautiful life and correspondence of her daughter, made a profound impression upon me. I had already "gone back to God," religion was dominating my thoughts more and more, I was grasping it

57-1090

internally as a sustaining force in my battle with myself as well as with socialism.

During all this speculative period I had been looking at the Christian claim that Jesus is of the Jews, was for the Jews first, as He was their Messiah. I found there was an agreement that Jesus was born of a Jewish mother, reared in a Jewish home, obeyed the Mosaic law and spoke as one who assumed to have greater authority than Moses. I set myself to the task of finding out, though there lurked in me a sense of fear that, if hearkened to, would have ended any further investigation. I realized that if Jesus were found to be the Messiah, I would be confronted with a responsibility requiring more resoluteness than I had to arouse, when faced with the question of leaving the socialist movement and the associations I had made therein. There always seemed to be a tempter in me, if I may personify it, who sent a sense of timidity, better perhaps fear, through me that I had to conquer before I could move. But move I always did, after arousing the will to follow my understanding rather than my feelings. The result was that I went ahead with my investigation and found the biblically recorded prophecies regarding the Messiah to have been fulfilled in Jesus.

The coming of the Messiah accounted for the end of the Aaronic priesthood, the sacrifice, and the Temple, for they were not in the divine plan of the New Dispensation, as will be shown later. Shorn of these essentials, what was left but to conclude that Judaism as a religion of God had fulfilled its mission?

To me, the end of Judaism did not mean that God had left man without a visible guide. I was convinced that dependence entirely upon the promptings of the heart for guidance is not a guarantee of certitude, so much needed in these days of religious and moral confusion. I was soon blessed with the conviction that the end of the covenant with an exclusive people, the chosen children of Israel, was followed by a new covenant, a covenant with all the people of all the world for all time. The evidence to me became conclusive that a new priesthood, a new sacrifice, in a new Church, had come into being. To me it was a God-made universal Church, divinely commissioned to teach by the Messiah who claimed to be "the way, and the truth and the life." (John XIV:6.)

All around me I saw Protestant churches that accepted Jesus as the Son of David, with members professing love of Him (which I did not question), and claiming their churches to be the Church of Christ. I found these churches to be, doctrinally, confusion—confounded. It was a veritable puzzle to see in the ministry so many educated men of differing beliefs, calling their contradictory churches—The Church. The very existence of them I found due primarily to differences regarding Christian teachings. Protestants themselves deplored the differences, which are greater today than they were while I was studying Protestantism.

Then, again, I found that Catholics affirm and Protestants deny that Christ established a visible church. To me, the claim of the Catholic Church seemed more reasonable. In fact, I found it easy to accept every one of the teachings of the Catholic Church I studied, so long as I could arrive at the point of accepting Jesus as the Christ. All her teachings appealed to me as following logically from that premise.

At last, I was determined to hesitate no longer. The words of Saul were in my heart—"Lord, what wilt Thou have me do?" The answer was plain: follow your conscience. I had long enough been an admirer of the Catholic Church aesthetically, doctrinally, sociologically and otherwise; the time had come to be one with Christ in her. The time for immediate action was at hand. A telephone call to Boston College placed me in touch with its president who set a time for my visit. There, at the appointed hour, I was placed in the care of Father Joseph H. Rockwell, S.J., and, after a few weeks of "instruction," or rather, examination as to my knowledge and acceptance of the teachings in the catechism, I was regenerated through the holy waters of baptism in the Immaculate Conception Church of Boston, on Sunday, May 21, 1905.

I had sought and found; knocked and the doors of real happiness were opened unto me. My experience was the story over again of the quest for the Holy Grail: a wanderer has searched afar for truth, battling against ignorance, temptation and sin, only to find that the Lord God loves him so that He has set His Church with the Sacred Vessel at his very door, the place from which he set out.

My conversion meant the end of my free-lance propaganda activity. The Catholic Church is one with St. Paul in holding it to be a usurpation to teach without being "sent" (Rom. X:15). It was Christ who sent His Apostles; and that authority has come down to our time through the bishops, their successors in the Catholic Church, and they delegate it to priests. Hence, to quote Pope Leo XIII, it is only as "echoes" of the bishops and priests that the laity may rightly take part publicly in teaching things Catholic.

After five years of public inactivity, the call came from His Grace, Archbishop (later Cardinal) William O'Connell, for service, to which it was a delight to respond. It was the beginning of an expression of confidence, on the part of Boston's Cardinal-Archbishop, in the sincerity of my desire to be of service to the Church, a desire which has continued ever since, and for which I thank God daily.

It was the inauguration of a series of public educational meetings to give workingmen an understanding of the basic principles that underlie the problems that affect their interests, to show them the value of the remedies the Church proposes, as well as to point out to them the shallowness and deceit of the proposals handed out by charlatans, who are often irreligious and anti-patriotic teachers.

During the year following, 1911, while working under the patronage of Archbishop O'Connell, a call came from the Central Bureau of the Central Verein, in St. Louis, Missouri, to take up work nationally in defense of the Church against the socialist propaganda which was making headway among Catholic workingmen. This call came through Mr. F. P. Kenkel, K.S.G., the Director of this German-Catholic federation, who was the leading sociologist among the Catholic laity of America. The invitation was an answer to six years of prayer for the opportunity to use my propaganda talents for the cause that was dear to my heart. So, despite there being no guarantee of a livelihood, I left my work at the bench and assumed the honor of being the first Catholic layman to devote full time to defending the Church against the socialist assault. The Central Bureau of the Central Verein arranged a schedule of twenty meetings in twenty cities. This was followed by a series of seventy additional addresses and quiz periods.

My purpose was to tell the public why the Catholic Church stands unitedly against doctrinaire socialism, and, while so doing, to prevent Catholics from being inveigled into socialism by exposing the specious arguments of its proponents. Especially was it to win misled Catholics back to their religious duties.

In the spring of 1914 I was called by the Knights of Columbus (as was Peter W. Collins, General Secretary of the Brotherhood of Electrical Workers) to take a leading part in the educational campaign of the organization. For six months a year, during a period of ten years, I addressed about fifteen hundred audiences in all parts of the United States and the Dominion of Canada on various phases of Socialism, Bolshevism, the Family, Peace and War, History In The Making, Red Mexico, and other allied subjects.

I entered the Catholic Church, as did my co-worker Martha Moore Avery, filled with a propaganda spirit which the socialist movement, false though it be in principle, instills into its members; a spirit worthy of a greater cause than the teachings of socialism represent; a spirit so greatly admired by me that my good feeling toward socialist propagandists has never waned, despite the many wicked things that they have said about me.

Looking over the propaganda field, discussing it with Martha Moore Avery, with whom I conferred on all matters of such a nature, I felt assured that the Church was failing to take advantage of a great opportunity, not merely to win outsiders, but to arouse the much-needed propaganda spirit among the laity. All around us could be seen every sort of ism, ology, sect; every kind of false theory and fanatical dream was being presented to the people gathered in the streets, squares and parks of the land. Why, then, are not Catholics, whose Church has within her keeping philosophical, religious and moral truth—whole and entire—presenting the principles, history and practices of their Church out in the open, in contrast to error, disruption and revolution? Why do not the Catholic laity carry on an open air counter-propaganda? I was simply enthused with the great opportunity that awaited Catholics, if they would only take advantage of it, to break down some of the barriers of misunderstanding and misrepresentation which are a hindrance to the gathering of a harvest of souls in America who, were they to know Catholic truth, would love it and work for its dissemination.

I was grateful for the opportunity, which finally came, to propagate the faith on the public platform, thanks to this Central Bureau of the Central Verein and the Knights of Columbus, but that did not fully satisfy my ambition. I wanted to give fuller expression to my propaganda spirit; I wanted to work where outsiders would more likely be attracted to the Catholic Church; I wanted to be a lay apostle to the man in the street.

It was the study of the encyclical on "The Duties of Christians as Citizens" that finally convinced my associate convert from Marx to Christ and me that our propaganda ambition was entirely in line with the teachings of the Church. Therein, Pope Leo XIII called for the utilization of the zeal of the laity for the propagation of the faith. Therein, was our warrant for looking forward confidently to the day when we would re-introduce street, square and park campaigning for Christ into the Catholic world.

It was on Boston Common that this apostolate started its activities and Boston Common has ever since been the main center of open air work while campaigning in and around the capital city of Massachusetts. There, the work began on Independence Day, 1917, when the Guild's Chaplain, Msgr. Michael J. Splaine, D.D., representing His Eminence, Cardinal O'Connell, was introduced by the chairman, Sergeant Arthur B. Corbett, to deliver the dedicatory address from the rostrum of the autovan.

The start had been made on a patriotic day on historic ground. The public press gave satisfactory reports and pictures of the occasion when the Catholic laity started out to win favor for their Church. We limited our first season to ninety days, during which time eighty open air meetings were addressed in and around Boston. Each meeting lasted from two to two and a half hours and ended with a quiz period. We addressed about 150,000 persons, who never before had heard the Catholic faith presented out in the open by laymen. In fact, many Catholics were so unacquainted with the history of the part that the laity had played, and are morally obligated to play in bringing Catholic truth to the uninformed, that they were amazed to know that Catholic laymen were permitted to do such work.

To our local success we desired to add a national demonstration of the practicability of carrying the Catholic message to the man in the street. This was due to an ardent desire to prove that the time was opportune for outdoor work, that a courteous hearing could be obtained for Catholic speakers in any city or town in the United States. We considered ourselves to be only pioneers who were "blazing the trail for others to follow," to quote the words of Bishop McGavick, of La Crosse, Wisconsin.

Success was assured when the bishops all along the line responded in a way that proved to us that the hierarchy were ready for the work. It has always been our policy to hold open air meetings only in those dioceses where the bishops give the work their approbation, and then to go only into those parishes where pastors express a willingness to have meetings within their jurisdictions.

I undertook this first cross-country tour of open air meetings in association with Arthur B. Corbett, as Martha Moore Avery limited her outdoor work to Boston and its environs. I was associated in tours, outside of Boston, with five of the many men who have played a part in outdoor work. They were:

ARTHUR B. CORBETT   *Boston, Mass.*
GEORGE R. MITCHELL   *Westminster, Md.*

WILLIAM E. KERRISH   *Boston, Mass.*
FRANCIS E. CAIN   *Somerville, Mass.*
THEODORE H. DORSEY   *Baltimore, Md.*

I may say, frankly, that without their aid, success would have been impossible. I am also indebted for success to the chaplain of the Boston group of outdoor speakers, Rev. Patrick J. Waters, Ph.D.

The ocean to ocean tour began with a meeting in the beautiful Civic Centre of San Francisco where an audience estimated at from six to seven thousand greeted us. The tour lasted two-thirds of a year, four months in California and four months of zigzagging across country, covering a distance of 13,000 miles.

I fully realize that there are times when silence is twice blessed, but during times when the moral standards which have made civilization possible are being questioned by some and utterly repudiated by others; when disruptive minorities are forcing the State to adopt measures that have a degenerating effect upon her citizens—I hold those to be the very times when the message of the Church should be re-echoed out in the open spaces. Thus could outsiders learn that the Catholic message alone contains the basic elements needed for the regeneration of man, for the regeneration and preservation of human society. Besides, no work more effectively stimulates the faith in the faithful, no work is more likely to make propagandists of the Catholic laity, than seeing and hearing their fellow-laymen presenting and defending things Catholic, out in the open, in a Catholic spirit.

My co-worker, Martha Moore Avery, died in 1929, which placed the responsibility of the work we had done jointly entirely upon me. We had been conducting the Common Cause Forum, a unique enterprise in that it was the only Catholic weekly forum in our country conducted in a large public auditorium and addressed by laymen only. It was distinctive because, of all the large Boston forums, it was the only one with a free platform. Discussion—pro and con—by persons in the audience followed every address instead of questions and answers. Mrs. Avery conducted the Common

Cause Forum alone while I was on the road; hence, at her death, I remained in Boston to carry on its interesting weekly meetings. Later on the Forum was closed, as I had resolved to devote all of my time to popularizing the lay apostolate to the man in the street, to which undertaking she and I were ardently devoted.

So I arranged a nationwide tour that would permit year-round open air meetings, six months in the northern and six months in the southern states. Before so doing, with the aid of Arthur B. Corbett, the young man with whom I made the ocean to ocean tour, some friends helped me to procure a new automobile, a large open car. It was a very attractive modern outfit, equipped with an amplifier, microphone and three horns. The horns were raised on a twelve foot mast, which was taken apart and placed in a box on the left side running board when not in use. It also had a mechanism for the electrical transmission of music. Thus the strains of "Agnus Dei," "Ave Maria," "The Palms," "The Holy City," and other Catholic hymns were heard by the motley crowds assembled in the highways and parks. The voices and music were sent out through the loud-speakers at distances that made it impossible to estimate the number who listened in, the unseen being sometimes larger than the seen audience.

The nationwide tour of open air meetings started on Sunday, June 14, 1931, from the beautiful grounds of St. Gabriel's Monastery and Retreat House in Brighton, Massachusetts, where the Passionist Fathers, their congregation, retreatants and others gave the campaigners a friendly and encouraging send-off.

The nationwide tour came to a halt, for a few months, at the end of 1935. During its four years, the message of Catholic truth had been carried to an average of twenty to twenty-five audiences a month, in thirty-one states. God alone knows the harvest of souls it has reaped. It has demonstrated the aid laymen can give to the Catholic cause by frankly, unequivocatingly, courteously making an intellectual and moral appeal to the diversified elements that gather in outdoor audiences.

No less than an average of fifty persons a year were brought to the baptismal font as a result of the tour, while it is impossible to estimate the number of fallen-aways induced to enter the tribunal of penance as a result of hearing their fellow-laymen out in the open, boldly talking Christ and His Church, and soliciting and answering all sorts of inquiries and objections promptly, pointedly and in a confident Christian spirit that counteracted misunderstanding and laid low error. Besides, the sale of over 40,000 cloth-bound copies of the *Campaigners for Christ Handbook* sent the message of the Church, in printed form, into many minds and homes where things Catholic never before found lodgement.

This pioneer nationwide Catholic outdoor campaign was intended to demonstrate and did demonstrate that the American field is ready to be ploughed, harrowed and planted by the laity with the seed of Catholic truth. It placed me in contact with a multitude of good folk outside the Church, who are sick of the long reign of the world, the flesh and the devil of modernism. I found them tired of the coarse, brutal and vile philosophy and practices which the Catholic Church alone has the principles, doctrinal unity and spiritual force to counteract. Many of them knew not what to do and where to go to get the peace, justice, love and hope their hearts yearned for. That is why they stood at open air meetings, courteously listening and simply amazed, for they were brought in varying degrees, and some of them said so frankly, to a realization that within the Church they disregarded there abides what alone will satisfy their hearts' longing. It requires courage to enter the Catholic Church, so I sincerely sympathized with them when told that their family ties and social standing kept them from entering. Surely, an army of the laity out in the open would be a tremendous power with which to overcome their failure to heed the words of our Lord, "He that loveth father or mother more than Me, is not worthy of Me, and he that loveth son or daughter more than Me, is not worthy of Me" (Matt. X:37).

The work has received the approbation of sixty dioceses in which open air meetings have been held. It has been crowned with the blessing of His Holiness, Pope Pius XI, who wrote,

through the then Papal Secretary of State, His Eminence,
Cardinal Pacelli—

> *"Dear Mr. Goldstein:*
>
> "His Holiness wishes me to express to you his apprecia-
> tion of the detailed account of the noble apostolate which
> you and your collaborators have been carrying on for
> years.
>
> "In pledge of abundant grace, the Holy Father sends
> to you and your colleagues the Apostolic Benediction,
> blessing at the same time the work to which you are
> dedicating yourself.
>
> "With sentiments of esteem and religious devotion,
> I am, my dear Mr. Goldstein,
>
> > "Sincerely yours in Christ,
> >
> > "CARDINAL PACELLI,
> >
> > > *"Secretary of State*
>
> "Vatican City,
> February 16, 1935."

The trail has been blazed, the field is white for a harvest of
souls; all that is needed is Catholic Action in the form of
campaigning for Christ.

My search for truth has been told in the foregoing pages. It
was truth eternal that I had to find, for that alone is un-
changeable truth, that alone is the same today as it was in the
infancy of the human race and as it will be even if this planet
upon which life's struggle goes on is no more. Thus I was
driven intellectually back to God. There arose within my
consciousness a realization of obligation to search into the
faith of my fathers for truth. There it was revealed by God,
there it was as the possession of the children of Israel, there
it was realized, elevated, personified in the Messiah, Jesus,
who said: "I am the truth."

To me the Catholic Church is the only thing worth living
and working for, and, if necessary, the greatest honor to die
for. All I ask of those who may profit by reading this autobiography is a prayer that I may persevere in the course I have
laid out for myself, along Catholic lines, until the end of my
days.

Seeds of Unity

ELIZABETH REID [1]

W HEN a bush fire rages through the gullies in Australia, it cracks open the hard seedcases of the wild flowers, and in the spring when the rains come there is an extraordinary abundance and variety of flowers.

It could be that the violent storms of evil which have raged over the world of the twentieth century have cracked open the hard "seedcases" of the laity. The many beautiful new developments in the lay apostolate seem to bear witness to this. When the blossoming time comes, the conversion of the world and the triumph of the Cross can be expected.

For me the first inkling of this new stirring in the Church came one evening just before World War II, when Dr. Lyd-

[1] Elizabeth Reid, Australian-born Grail leader, has pioneered since 1948 as a lay missioner in Hong Kong. Head of the Hong Kong Grail team, editor of the Catholic paper, and N.C.W.C. correspondent, Miss Reid has traveled widely in Asia, and has covered with camera and pen many important events in recent Asian history: the exchange of prisoners in Korea, the siege of Dien Bien Phu and Hanoi in Viet Nam, the Bandung-Asian Congress in Indonesia, the Asian lay apostolate congress in Manila. At the Grail Center in Taikoo-Lau Village outside Hong Kong, she has given a warm welcome and often a home to young women refugees from communist China. Here too she has organized training courses in the lay apostolate for students and working girls of the city, helping them to play their part in the great upsurge of the Faith in Hong Kong today.

Miss Reid has just completed a lecture tour in the United States, and she is now on the staff of the Grail Institute for Overseas Service, which was opened at 308 Clinton Avenue, Brooklyn 5, New York, in October, 1956. The Institute is preparing American young women for active service as lay workers on the mission frontiers of the Church.

wine van Kersbergen, a Grail leader, was showing a movie in Brisbane, Australia, of 10,000 Dutch Grail members in a mass play. They were praying around a huge, brightly-colored cross in the Olympic Stadium in Amsterdam, communicating their spirit and conviction to some 40,000 onlookers.

The impact of that movie shattered my hitherto peaceful existence in the remote island continent where I was born. Australia *is* indeed off the beaten track, "down under" from the surging currents of world affairs. I had lived outside the city in our family home, high on a hill with no near neighbors, and attended the same school all my life. My journalist father was a delightful companion to walk and read with, and my mother, who loved and cared for all of us, was always available. Up until this time, swimming in the river, playing tennis or golf, grooming my dog, studying, going to parties, discussing books and Australian nationalism filled my days. Then suddenly this staggering new idea that the conversion of the whole world concerned *me*. I had a vague idea that the Cross and sacrifice were involved in it somewhere, but at eighteen the only tangible knowledge of sacrifice I had was to go without sweets during Lent!

A few weeks later a letter came in the post from the secretary of the Grail inviting me to take part in a summer school in Sydney, 600 miles south from my home. And so "the journey of a thousand miles began with a single step," as I heard years later from a Chinese philosopher in Taiwan. Girls came from all parts of Australia to the summer school, and the idea of the lay apostolate, of one's personal responsibility for the growth of the Mystical Body, of the need for training to take one's place in the ranks of the Church, began to take shape. For the first time in my life I took part in a dialogue Mass, and it began to dawn on me that the sacrifice of Calvary is the focal point in history, and that the Mass in my parish church each day *is* Calvary projected into time. The Cross and sacrifice began to make sense. A whole new vision began to unfold before my eyes: a vision of woman's talents, of her special capacity for sacrifice and self-giving, of the Cross as the deepest inspiration for a woman's heart and the climax of the message we modern lay apostles were called to bring.

It was in the early 1920's that five young women studying under a great professor (Dr. Jacques van Ginneken, S.J.) at the Catholic University of Nymegen in Holland came to the idea, with him, of a modern woman's movement, a movement of *lay* women living in the world, using all the freedom and opportunities which life today offers women to help draw society toward God. Thousands upon thousands of girls responded to this idea—first in Holland, then in Germany, Great Britain, Australia, America. Students, teachers, office and factory workers, artists, musicians, writers, nurses—girls in all walks of life united their talents and energies in a vigorous apostolic movement, inspired by a positive and profound concept of woman's specific role in the plan of redemption. The variety of their activities was sometimes bewildering —mass plays in which thousands took part, publications, radio programs, films, exhibits, social services, apostolic campaigns, training courses for lay leadership—but underneath all the activities, the one goal: through the womanly talent for sacrifice and self-giving to bring a dynamic Christian spirit into all avenues of modern life. And at the heart of the movement, a permanent nucleus of laywomen, giving their entire lives to provide a basis of unity and a guarantee of spiritual strength for the whole.

For me, the vision grew and deepened. I saw that being used for the conversion of the world in this time was not a girl's dream, something to be got at bargain prices, but a tremendous task, something for which to give one's whole life. I joined the Grail nucleus, and in the training years that followed I learned how rich and full is our life in Christ, that life we are called to share with all men everywhere.

From its beginning, the Grail had a threefold aim: (1) to prepare Catholic young women for lay leadership in Christianizing their own environment; (2) to work among non-Catholics, to break down prejudice and draw them toward the Church; (3) to work among women in mission lands, helping to build the missionary Church and to develop local lay leaders.

After World War II time was ripe to carry out this last cherished plan of sending lay apostles to the missions. Grail teams went forth, to Hong Kong and Indonesia in Asia, to Brazil and Surinam in South America, to Uganda, the Belgian Congo, Basutoland, Egypt, the Union of South Africa. Team members work as nurses, doctors, teachers, social workers, journalists, helping to meet some of the urgent needs of the Church in these areas, helping too to train the local young women for their part in the lay apostolate.

I was one of the fortunate ones who overflowed from my own country to a neighboring place. After five years on the staff of the Grail Adult Education Centre, "Tay Creggan" in Melbourne, and three years as editor of *Torchlight,* a national Catholic girls' magazine, I was assigned to Hong Kong.

It was 1948 when I landed on that small island off the coast of China—just before the advance of Mao Tse-tung made of Hong Kong a solitary island of freedom set in a sea of communism. During the seven years which followed I was editor of *The Sunday Examiner,* the diocesan Catholic weekly. As well, I have had assignments as an N.C.W.C. newspaper correspondent and photographer, which took me to Korea and Japan, Formosa and the Philippines, Viet Nam, Malaya, Indonesia, Melville and Bathurst Islands, and Fiji.

As the method of The Grail is to form "centres of Christian life" adapted to the needs of each area, where the spirit of the Gospel can be lived by young women and integrated into the social structures and institutions of modern life, our team in Hong Kong opened a hostel for refugee students in 1949. In this small house overlooking the bay, I have lived and worked with American, Dutch, Chinese and Australian Grail workers. Making up our household have been young daughters of China, from the northern stretches of Ninghsia, from Peking, Mukden, Shanghai and Canton—fleeing the tide of communism. They managed to seep into Hong Kong across shallow border marshes; slipping over the sides of sampans and swimming ashore; month after month arriving in the loaded trains which pulled into Lo-Wu at the Chinese-British border. They came from the shelter of decent homes to the swift moving cosmopolitan life of Hong Kong. We counted among us one whose father was killed by Communists because he was a landowner; two sisters forced to join the Young Pioneers League of the Communist Party, and smuggled over the border by an aged grandmother after months of hiding and hardships; dozens who saw their Catholic University closed, their professors humiliated and imprisoned and who, rather than submit to learning without truth, came destitute to Hong Kong. In China, they had seen an international anti-God force at work; in Hong Kong they realized the worldwide mission of Christianity. They had seen and had suffered the corruption and poisoning of young minds; now they understood better the importance of their task as Christian women to bring life.

As I write, so many faces pass before me—eager people and tired ones—longing and seeking for truth, torn this way and that with ideas which are alien to their culture and understanding. People met on roads, in the paddies and sah-wahs, in busses and trains, flying over devastated countries, people waiting for friends to stand beside them in these changing days. People who need some of us physically among them, all of us spiritually. How many of us could be used there?

Millions of Asian people are groaning under the weight of exile, as refugees cut off from their cities and towns and villages by communism. They have come as far as they can come in Hong Kong, Korea and Viet Nam. Behind the bamboo curtain many millions more have been subjected to the ideas of materialism and all the other evil doctrines that are now being widely diffused. The Communists have taken advantage of the poverty, of the nationalistic upsurge, which they have used as a springboard to enslave vast sectors of Asia, and have subjected the people to previously unheard-of torments and persecutions.

Because it is difficult to imagine just how deeply the Cross is being lived out by our Asian brothers and sisters in this time, I will give two concrete examples.

This happened in Pusan, Korea, at a clinic for refugees. All day I had worked there with my camera getting pictures and human interest stories which could be used in America for a

drive for War Relief Services-N.C.W.C. In the late afternoon
returning to the lane to see how many people were still waiting, I saw one woman huddled near a wall with a grey-
blanketed bundle hugged to her breast. She kept peering at
her burden, and I became curious to see why she was so
concerned. I tugged at the blanket, and she looked up at me
with such a longing in her eyes that I pulled a little harder.
A child of about three years covered with smallpox, not a
sound spot on the whole body or face, was revealed. A slit for
the child's mouth breathed out hot gasps of breath over a
black hard tongue, like a sun-dried piece of wet leather—and
all I had was a camera. It could not heal, it could only record
this misery. The nurse came, but it was too late to do anything
to help the child, and the supply of penicillin had run out.
Water was brought to moisten the child's mouth and later
some rice for the mother. Then this refugee woman went
back in the dusk to her home on the street with her precious
bundle—baptized now, another Christ filling up in his tiny
body what is wanting to the conversion of the world in our
time. I turned to go back to the correspondent's billet. The
doctor in charge walked with me to the gate. We heard a faint
cry, and I saw her stoop and pick up a tiny abandoned baby
which must have been left in the corner of the lane. She
looked worn and grey, but when I saw her lift that scrap of
humanity to her cheek, then gather it under her coat to make
it warm, I saw in a little minute Christ's love, Christ's passion
being lived out now, and I knew surely that all the toil and
suffering of the people in that alley, and all the toil of the
nurses and doctors with too much to do, were part of the
redeeming Cross in our time.

This time the scene is Viet Nam. I was on my way to get
pictures in the camps of the 800,000 refugees from North
Viet Nam who are now living outside Saigon. It is something
I can never forget as I stood on a hill that morning and looked
down on the waterless, dust-blown tract of land with its
sagging tents and forest of crosses rough hewn and lashed
together with reeds. It was Passion Week and the Cross has

never been more real, more royal, and by the end of that day, more than I have ever known before, a symbol of hope.

To keep their Faith alive—that is what spurred these predominantly Christian people to uproot themselves from home, village and countryside, from the little fields they have tilled for generations, from churches where their relatives had suffered martyrdom for the Faith, from all the familiar things man holds so dear. They left everything because they knew that life under the Vietminh—communism—would mean a godless education for their children, a life without priests to administer the sacraments and to offer the sacrifice of the Mass. Now on the arid, sun-parched ground of their campsites around Saigon, they are gathered under the shadow of their crosses—a people magnificent in their poverty, splendid in their faith, in whose sign of the cross they will surely conquer.

Looking out over those miles of refugee huts with their crosses, I thought of the movie I had seen long ago in Brisbane of the Grail play, "The Royal Road of the Cross," and the sharp impact upon me of those thousands of eager young faces, proclaiming their conviction, "In the Cross is life, in the Cross is joy of spirit." It came in a flash—the height and depth and breadth of our vocation in the Grail, especially in this time. I thought too of the cross on the hill at Grailville, our training center in the United States, and the cross on the jagged rock in the mountains of Australia, set there by young Australians who have seen the same ideal as their counterparts across the Pacific; and a third cross, built into the wall of our international Grail Training Center in Holland. An external symbol, but one which unites lay apostles in Europe, America, Australia, with their sisters over the earth, a sign of our deep will to give ourselves for the building of Christ's Kingdom.

This is the eternal *now* to strengthen Christ's Kingdom in Asia. Missionaries there are generally conscious that a crisis of a special sort is upon them and many see that their hope lies in the lay apostolate. They need lay leaders from overseas to share with the local people the responsibility of the specific lay contribution in establishing, developing, and consolidating the Church "while it is still day." They need people with profes-

sional skills—teachers, doctors, nurses, journalists, home econo-
mists, social workers, artists, but most of all people with hearts
capable of love and service, people who are willing to trade
with their talents for the big bargain of the conversion of the
world.

To help meet this need, an Institute for Overseas Service has
begun functioning in Brooklyn, New York. At this Grail
Center, American young women can prepare for service in
helping to build the Church overseas. Here, under leading
mission authorities, they can study the position of the Church
in the world today, the special needs and problems of the
different areas, and the adaptation of Christian principles in
the various cultures. Here they can become acquainted with
the basic ideas and methods of the modern lay apostolate. And,
most important of all, they can deepen their own life in
Christ, their grasp of the "Good Tidings," their power of
prayer, their practice of the Christian virtues. After training,
they can pledge themselves for a limited term of service—
three to five years; or they can dedicate their entire lives to
work overseas as permanent members of the Grail nucleus.

So today, full-time members of the Grail from Europe,
America, and Australia can be seen working hand-in-hand
with young women of Asia, Latin America, and Africa. They
are striving to nurture a seed of Christian thought and action,
a seed which can bring forth fruit in the spirit of the Cross in
a world which has rejected the Cross, because in the last resort
"the hope of the world rests on the existence of a spiritual
nucleus of believers who are the bearers of the seed of unity."

Money and Us

MARGARET M. THOMPSON [1]

PERHAPS the title of this article should be "Money and Me" instead of "Money and Us." Although the general considerations I have set down here apply, I believe, to anyone, still I write as a single working woman with no dependents. Were I to marry and acquire a family, the proportions of my income spent for rent, clothes and so on, and a program of savings and contributions would change. But because there are so many women in circumstances similar to mine, and because money, its getting and spending, is something we should all give ample thought to, I write as I do.

Money is important because without what it buys, we might exist, but we cannot really live. Money is also important because it exerts a major influence upon our lives, both in its getting and in its spending. It can be productive of much good or of much evil. Money is neither good nor evil in itself but it produces one or the other. Money troubles plague many marriages. Legacies disposing of wealth can divide families by bitter feelings. Wealth can be used to spread goodwill between nations or it can promote the rivalries that bring about war. Someone wiser than I said to me once, "Money and sex cause more difficulties for people than any other factors of life. If

---

[1] Margaret M. Thompson, a federal employee in a large American city, regards her earnings as belonging entirely to God for use according to His will. Her concept of personal poverty is reminiscent of the Christ-like spirit of St. Francis of Assisi and presents a refreshing contrast to the materialism and self-seeking so characteristic of our time.

we have not found an answer for the problems they create in our own life, we have not found a way to help other people."

The first part of the money problem is getting it! Leaving aside the consideration of "ill-gotten gains," getting it means for the majority of us that someone hires the use of our skills and abilities and time, and at stated intervals we receive some money in return. That is all there is to it. Simple, isn't it?

Oh, but it is not so simple, if we are seriously attempting to live as Christians. Money may be a material means of exchange but it can take on a spiritual value that carries over into its use. I earn my money by working at a "job." If that job is the one God wants me to have, is part of His plan for me, if it is one in which I can and do use the talents, skills, intelligence, and all else He gave me, then the pay I receive for my work takes on a sacred quality. My *attitude* toward work in general, and toward my job in particular, in other words my *philosophy* of work, if it be a Christian philosophy, will also add spiritual value to my earnings. If I do my God-given work as He wants me to *for His sake,* then, in a sense, I have "doubled my money."

Granting all that, how do I regard my money? Do I think of it as all mine, to spend (or save) as I please? Or do I adopt the Old Testament teaching of tithing, as do some modern Christians, giving one-tenth of my income to the Church or other religious or worthy agencies? I tried tithing once upon a time, on a very small salary, and it was an amazing experience. I think it is a good practice, certainly as a beginning lesson in the Christian use of money, but tithing is as "milk for babies." I believe that with spiritual maturity our means should be regarded as belonging entirely to God, to be used as we honestly think He wants us to use them.

So then, what do I do about my money? I suppose the orthodox answer to that should be, "First make a budget." Personally I am in favor of budgets, but each of many budgets I have drawn up was wrecked beyond repair by some emergency. Even so, I have a budget of sorts, a six-column affair, the columns labeled respectively "Rent," "Meals," "Bus fare," "Batteries" (for a most necessary hearing aid), "Church and missions," and a sixth very wide column labeled "for-whatever-can-be-covered-by-whatever-is-left-over-when-bed-board-bus-batteries-and-Church-are-taken-care-of."

Budget or not, necessity is usually the foremost factor governing our spending. We all need food, clothes, shelter. Most of us need transportation to and from work. Those needs can be met frugally or moderately, or they can expand into luxury items, depending on our standards and desires, but we know how much our pay *must* cover.

The next factor governing spending is our desires, which include our standard of living. Our needs and desires can be synonymous, but they seldom are. Our standard of living depends partly on our childhood environment and partly on our present one. A working girl from a poverty-stricken home may consider a rented furnished room in a modest home almost like heaven; a working girl from a wealthy home, who works because she wants something to keep her occupied, and who lives in a swanky apartment, would "simply die" if she had to live in the kind of room her poorer sister enjoys.

Our standards of living and our desires are also affected by the way our neighbors live. We want to keep up with the Joneses. Advertising and window dressing, both of which have been developed into a fine art, also affect our standards and whet our desires, by suggesting that "this is just what you need."

The difference between a need and a desire is pointed up by an incident involving a friend of mine. She and another girl recently went to the bank at lunch time. They stopped to look at some dresses in a shop window and the girl said, "Let's go in and look at them. They are only twelve-fifty." But my friend demurred, saying "I don't need a dress right now." The other girl, shocked, exclaimed, "Do you only buy dresses when you *need* them?"

The way we use our money is governed by some of our character traits, and can therefore be revealing to us and to such of our friends as know our acts and their motives. One trait it reveals is the degree of our faith, or its negative opposite, fear. Do I save every cent I can, so I will not have a penniless old age? Or do I spend as I think God wants me to spend, even to the last cent, perhaps, trusting Him to provide for my needs? I must say I have only observed one case of extreme penny-pinching in my time, but I think fear of an impoverished old age haunts even many "good Christians."

For my own old age, I have the feeling that I won't have any. (I hope I am wrong.) Some of us won't. A common way of providing for our old age is by saving some of our income. Personally, every time I try to save, an emergency comes up that knocks my bank balance back to zero. As a Federal employee, I participate in the compulsory savings program known as the Retirement Plan. Right now I also have a small savings account besides. (Some of my friends would be shocked speechless if they knew just *how* small it is!) What I am saving it for I do not yet know, except that I believe God wants me to save it. Sometimes a doubt of my own common sense creeps in when I realize that I do not by now have thousands of dollars accumulated. And then I read and ponder again what Christ said about not laying up for ourselves treasure upon earth, and I wonder if He would not like to see many more of us taking that literally.

Our use of money is also regulated by our sense of values. I go into the dime store and see earrings on the jewelry counter that I like and could use as a change from the few I already possess. They are only thirty-nine cents. And then I think of how many days that thirty-nine cents could feed a child in one of our mission fields. Which do I value more, my own adornment or the welfare of a little child? If I value a fat savings account and the freedom from worry about the future that I think it will bring, I save every cent I can. If I value the good opinion of others, I put my money into anything I think will win that from them, be it clothes, other possessions, promotions, or whatever.

Finally, a sense of responsibility, which any mature, informed and thoughtful person has, enters into our spending. It is more than impulsive generosity. No one of us can meet all the needs of the world. But if I assume such material responsibility as I can for a few, or even one, of my brothers or sisters, then I have reason to believe and the right to pray that other needy ones will be helped by those among whom God apportions the responsibility.

If I am responsible, I realize how vast is our wealth here in America, compared with that of other nations and people. I am only an American by accident of birth. I have no inherent right to so much more of this world's goods than most people of the world ever have had or ever will have. I could have been born in one of the countries where people live on a bare subsistence level. Or I could have been born among those who had good homes and good positions taken from them and who now wander over the face of the earth, destitute and homeless—the "displaced."

All that I have been saying here about money comes out of my own convictions and practices of many years. I'd like to take the liberty of being personal for a few moments. I am a classified Federal employee, grade four, single and with no dependents. My only income is my salary. I rent a small room, with breakfast provided, in the home of friends, and although in a sense I have the run of the house, still it is just a rented room.

For many years I have given money toward religious causes. Two years ago I became a Catholic, and in appreciation of that tremendous gift of the Faith, I gave quite a bit, proportionately, to my Church. Because I realize what the Catholic Faith can mean to individuals and to the world, I desire to do all I can to aid its spread. After some thought, I decided that the maximum use for what little money I may leave when I die would be for the education of candidates to the priesthood, those who could not pursue their studies without financial help from outside their families.

Over a year ago I made a will to that effect. However, it may be (I hope it is) a long time before I die, and priests are needed *now*, so I decided I should not wait but could and should do something about it now. So I "adopted" a seminarian in a Near East mission seminary, paying his modest tuition costs in installments for his last six years of study. (I was alerted to such a need by the "Catholic Near East" column in *Our Sunday Visitor*.) Last fall, after a sizable pay raise, I adopted another seminarian, and I pay so much a month for each of them.

About the time I adopted my second "son," the annual special collection for the Society for the Propagation of the Faith was taken up, and in my parish church we were told that in 1954, American Catholics gave an average of *twenty-six cents apiece* to the missions. That figures out as one penny every other Sunday! It really shocked me, but perhaps what I can give compensates in some small measure for those who cannot give much, and can help make reparation for those who can give and will not.

Friends sometimes say to me, "Why don't you get an apartment of your own?" or "Why don't you buy a car? You'd have lots of fun with one." And lately I got to wondering if I were just being foolish, so I prayed for an answer to the question of my giving. I don't mind *appearing* foolish but I want to *be* sensible. No, "sensible" is not the word, for it connotes "doing the way everyone else does," or "getting some fun out of life" or "saving up for your old age." I want to do the *God-willed* thing. So, soon after I prayed about it, I came across Christ's words again, "For he who would save his life will lose it; but he who loses his life for my sake and for the gospel's sake will save it." For the first time I saw that as applying to my money. Isn't money, or what we secure with money, an integral part of life?

This revelation of what I do with my money is going to make good material for an argument, should some of my friends happen to read this. Once I told a broker friend how I felt about money and how I used mine, and he began to look worried. Finally he blurted, to my amusement, "But what if you die? How will your burial expenses be paid?" I could assure him that he would not have to pass the hat for me because I carried enough life insurance (compulsory in the firm I then worked for) to take care of any reasonable expenses.

Someone says "apartment" to me, and the old longing for a place I can call mine sweeps back over me. Then I think of the hordes of homeless ones in the world today and I know that it simply does not matter whether or not I have my own place in which to live. Certainly I know that I cannot both contribute to the spread of the Faith and have that apartment, not in my town where rents are extremely high. And certainly I am suffering no deprivation, so I can offer up that perfectly legitimate desire of mine for the sufferings of those made homeless by the cruelty of man to man.

As I write these words, the conviction comes to me again, as it has before, that although I do give much in proportion to what I have, I still do not give to the uttermost farthing, to help feed, clothe, house or educate my needy brother or sister. Some of my money still is spent greedily and some of it thoughtlessly. I know that on Judgment Day, my Judge will point His finger at those greedy expenditures, and He will say, "What do you have to say about those?" And I will only be able to answer, "Lord, I'm sorry—I just didn't think."

Money can be blessed, and can carry a blessing from those who have to those who have not. And as we give, so will we care, for it is true that "Where your treasure is, there will your heart be also." And as we care more, so will we give more, for the reverse is also true, "Where your heart is, there will your treasure be also."

The Vocation to Politics

EUGENE J. MC CARTHY [1]

Iɴ ᴀ democracy every citizen possesses political power and therefore each citizen carries a corresponding responsibility. He is called, in a sense, to carry out these responsibilities. Not every citizen has a vocation to political office. The manner and measure of participation in politics varies from individual to individual and depends on personality as well as conditions of history, professional and family obligations, and other qualifying circumstances. There is no excuse for complete neutralism and detachment.

The Christian must assume his civic responsibilities as a citizen, and more particularly as a Christian citizen. He cannot, as Charles Williams, an Anglican writer, has pointed out, be indifferent to so important an area of conflict as that of politics, since politics is one of the areas in which the conflict between good and evil is waged, and great advantage is given to evil by neglect. Pope Pius XII has stated the same thought in more detail. The Christian citizen, he said, must be actively present in political life "wherever vital interests are at stake; where laws concerning the worship of God, marriage, the family, the schools, the social order are being deliberated. . . ."

---

[1] Eugene J. McCarthy is now serving his fourth term as United States Representative for the Fourth District of the State of Minnesota. He frequently contributes articles to Catholic and secular periodicals and in 1955 he was the recipient of the Cardinal Newman Award, which is conferred annually for outstanding service to the Newman Clubs throughout the country. Mr. McCarthy's own philosophy is admirably expressed in this splendid study of the Christian in politics.

The Christian who undertakes to fulfill his civic responsibilities needs to give some preliminary thought to the basic questions concerning the nature and functions of government. In this century, and more immediately in this generation, the power of the absolute state—ruthless, self-justifying, ignoring the rights of persons and of other institutions such as the family and the Church—has been forcefully demonstrated. We have learned a lesson which we should not soon forget. We have learned that we must at all times be alert to the danger of the intrusion of the state into areas of culture and into areas in the social and private life of man which are beyond the authority of the state. In our alertness and vigilance, however, we should not be led to accept unsound theories concerning the origin, nature, functions, and purposes of the state. What is called for is careful examination, distinction, and re-ordination.

American political thought has been strongly influenced by an erroneous, pessimistic concept of the nature and functions of the state. Thomas Paine gave the first native expression to this viewpoint about the time that the Declaration of Independence was drawn. Then he wrote: "Government, like dress, is the badge of lost innocence. The palaces of kings are built upon the ruins of the bowers of Paradise." And again: "Were the impulses of conscience clearly and irresistibly obeyed, man would need no other law-giver." His thought is in the tradition of Hobbes, who held that man is driven by reckless pursuit of selfish interests and that government is simply a contractual substitute, a state of affairs in which man lives in continuous fear of attack and death. The state, according to this pessimistic theory, arises from the evil or depraved nature of man, and, moreover, this evil and depraved nature is the lasting justification of the state.

It is important to note that this unsound theory of the state has its theological element. The erroneous doctrine that original sin has utterly corrupted human nature buttresses the false philosophical concept.

Of course, the state does have a function which is the result of the disorder in human nature—the consequence of the fact of evil. The state must defend human society from the most concrete and obvious forms of evil or injustice. This social evil is expressed in three general forms, or at three levels: at the international level, when one nation seeks to destroy or seriously interfere with the national independence of another; at the civil level, when some social class or institution violates the rights of persons or of other classes or institutions in society; and at the criminal level, when an individual openly rebels against the general order by committing crime.

But this negative, protective function is not the only justification for government, that is, for the state. It is not even the fundamental one. Man needs the state and this need is not the consequence of natural depravity, nor of the fall of Adam, or original sin. Neither does it depend on the relative goodness or badness of the mass of mankind at any particular period of history. Man's need for the state rests in his rational, social nature. This need would remain even though man had never fallen. It remains also for man redeemed by grace, for grace does not destroy nature or make essential social or political institutions, such as the family and the state, unnecessary. A society of saints, if they drove automobiles, would present the problem of whether they should pass on the right or on the left side of the road.

In addition to this negative function of preventing and counteracting evil, the state has a positive function: namely, to assist man in the pursuit of happiness in the temporal order. This does not mean that the state is indifferent to the absolute, but simply that its immediate and direct purpose is the temporal good of man, the human good, that which is generally referred to as the common good.

This common good includes three principal categories of human good things:

First, those material goods which are necessary to maintain life and necessary as material helps to intellectual, moral, and spiritual growth.

Second, those intellectual goods, the knowledge and culture of the mind, which liberate man from ignorance and false fear.

Third, moral goods, or moral goodness, the mastery of self,

the possession of those virtues which in the limited order of temporal life are the highest goal—the good life described and sought after by the Greek philosophers.

Knowledge of political theory, in itself, is not enough. The Christian citizen must make application of his knowledge. He must participate in the political life of his community, province, state, and nation. He should, in fulfillment of his minimum obligations, have some knowledge of major candidates and major issues, and he should vote in principal elections. Beyond this he must give consideration to participation in party politics, in campaigns, and to holding party or government offices.

The Christian, in approaching politics, must remember that politics is part of a real world. He must be realistic, anticipating that in that world the simple choice between that which is altogether good and that which is altogether bad is seldom given. The ideal is seldom realized and often cannot be advocated. Trade, diplomatic relations and cooperation with nations whose conduct we condemn may be made necessary by circumstances. Political leaders may, in what Maritain describes as a regressive or barbarous society, have their freedom of choice reduced to the point where they must take a position which is questionable rather than the alternative which is simply and completely bad. Prudence may require the toleration of evil in order to prevent something worse. It may dictate a decision to let the cockle grow with the wheat.

Politicians are expected to compromise, yet they are ordinarily criticized for being compromisers. The writings of Machiavelli, together with all the associations that go with his name, have placed a burden upon politics and politicians. Compromise is the mark of human relations, not only in politics, but in almost every institution or social relationship involving two or more persons. Genuine compromise is not a violation of principle, not a compromise with principle, but with reality.

Lord Morley has well defined its nature: In his essay, "Compromise," he states that the interesting and basic question really involved in compromise is not one of principle against principle, but one that turns upon the placing of the boundary that divides wise suspense in forming opinions, wise reserve in expressing them, and wise tardiness in trying to realize them, from unavowed disingenuousness, from self-delusion, from voluntary dissimulation, ignorance, and pusillanimity.

The fact that politics does involve difficult choices and compromises does not make it bad in itself. Thomas More, writing in *Utopia,* expressed the idea in these words: "If evil opinion and naughty persuasion cannot be utterly and altogether plucked out of their hearts; if you cannot, even as you would, remedy vices which habit and custom have confirmed, yet this is no cause for leaving and forsaking the Commonwealth."

. The Christian who turns to politics must be on guard against an error of another kind, the error of confusing politics and its secular content and purposes with religion. There have been many Christian political thinkers and leaders who have attempted to define and to realize what they considered to be the ideal Christian state. Some have seen the ideal in the medieval synthesis of State and Church and looked to the restoration of a similar order today. For others, the ideal Christian state is conceived as a monarchy with the Christian monarch defending both faith and country. Others envision the Christian state as a democracy founded upon the natural law.

If the concept of Christian politics is to be justified, or if any historical state is to merit the label "Christian," it must be of such kind that, as Franz Joseph Schöningh, editor of *Hochland,* points out in the April, 1949, issue of that magazine, "fundamentally, through its Christian character alone, it differs from every other."

Neither history nor political theory establishes any basis for the application of the label "Christian" in any absolute sense to politics. Recognition of Christianity by the state does not make the state itself "Christian," nor does official approval of certain Christian forms and practices. Neither does the fact that all citizens of a state are Christians make that state a

Christian state. A government might be distinguished as more or less Christian to the degree that it has either succeeded or failed in establishing a greater measure of justice; or, a form of government might be called Christian to the extent that it depends, as does democracy, upon the inspiration of the Gospels for its fulfillment. Such qualified application sets the limits of the use of the word "Christian."

Although the existence of a purely Christian politics cannot be established, there remains an obvious need for Christians in politics—that is, for Christian politicians, and it should be possible to distinguish these Christians in politics. If such distinction could not be made there would be no point in urging the participation of Christians in political life.

What are the marks of a Christian politician—plain citizen or officeholder? He is not necessarily the one who is seen most often participating in public religious activities or regularly conferring with religious leaders. He need not be a "leading layman." He is not necessarily the one who first and most vociferously proclaims that his position is the Christian one, and who attempts to cover himself and his cause with whatever part of the divided garment is within his reach. He is not necessarily the one who makes of every cause a "crusade," presenting himself, as Carlyle described the crusader, as "the minister of God's justice, doing God's judgment on the enemies of God."

The Christian in politics should be judged by the standard of whether through his decisions and actions he has advanced the cause of justice and helped at least to achieve the highest degree of perfection possible in the temporal order. He should know and understand the great body of teachings on secular matters available to him and should seek to apply them.

When a political problem can be reduced to a simple question of feeding the hungry or of not feeding them; of ransoming the captive or of refusing to ransom him; of harboring the harborless, or of leaving him homeless—there should be no uncertainty as to the Christian position. Problems of overpopulation, or displaced and expelled peoples, of political refugees, and the like are in reality not always reducible to simple choices. As a general rule the inclinations of the Christian should be to liberality. His mistakes and failures on problems of this kind should be the consequences of leniency rather than of fearful self-interest; of excess of trust, rather than of excessive doubt and anxiety.

The Christian politician should, of course, hold fast to the moral law, remembering that the precepts of morality do not themselves change, even though the way in which they are applied to concrete acts may be modified as society regresses or is perverted. On the basis of moral principles, he must strive to separate good from bad even though the line may be blurred or shifting.

He must remember and honor in action the rule that the end does not justify the means. He should carefully avoid confusion such as that which is manifest in Cromwell's reply to Wharton's protest of Pride's Purge and the execution of the King: "It is easy to object to the glorious actings of God, if we look too much upon the instruments. Be not offended at the manner. Perhaps there was no other way left."

The Christian in politics should be distinguished by his alertness to protect and defend the rights of individuals, or religious and other institutions from violation by the state, by other institutions, or by persons. He should be the first to detect and oppose a truly totalitarian threat or movement and the last to label every proposal for social reform—totalitarian.

He should protect the name of Christ from abuse and profanation, and should himself avoid unwarranted appeals to religion. He has a very special obligation to keep the things of God separate from those of Caesar.

The Christian in politics should shun the devices of the demagogue at all times, but especially in a time when anxiety is great, when tension is high, when uncertainty prevails, and emotion is in the ascendency. The Christian in politics should speak the truth. He should make his case in all honesty—aware that any other action is, as C. S. Lewis states, to offer to the Author of all truth the unclean sacrifice of a lie. He should not return calumny and slander in the same token, but combat them with truth and honesty, risking defeat for the sake of truth. He should not resort to the common practice of labelling, which by its falseness violates justice, and by its indignity offends charity. Powerful personalities may be able to stand against these forces; the weak are likely to be destroyed. It is these who must be the concern of Christians.

The task of the politician is a humble one. His work is not at the level of the philosopher, the theologian, or the moralist, but it is the rather more menial work of putting the determinations of the philosophers, the theologians, and the moralists into effect. The politician, of course, should be a theologian, a philosopher and a moralist himself, and he should listen to the voice of these disciplines. As he proceeds in action, his general guide must be to make his decisions in the hope that they may help to make an imperfect world somewhat more perfect, or that, at least, if he cannot make an imperfect world more perfect, he can save it from becoming less perfect or finally from becoming entirely evil and perverted. He can try to prevent degradation; to prevent decline; and, if possible, he can hope to move things forward and upward toward right and justice. That is the purpose and the end of political action and of the compromises that go with such action.

These seem difficult standards and demands and their fulfillment requires sanctity. There is, however, no other measure which is valid for Christians in politics or for Christians in any other way of life. As the great politician and saint Thomas More observed: "It is not possible for all things to be well, unless all men are good—which I think will not be this good many years."

Every Christian an Apostle

DOROTHY DOHEN [1]

IT MADE me happy to come across recently in Monsignor G. Philips' admirable book, *The Role of the Laity in the Church,* the statement that "the word 'lay' originally meant 'sacred' or 'baptized.'" In the early days of the Church, especially by St. Paul, the word "laos" was used to identify the holy people of God, the members of the new Christian community, sanctified by faith and baptism. Therefore, following this ancient usage, the *lay* man is a person "consecrated," set apart for a holy purpose—"even though," as Monsignor Philips remarks, "the holy things are especially entrusted to the clergy."

I repeat, it made me happy to read all this, because I think there are two areas of confusion regarding lay people. The first involves the feeling, which some clergy and faithful still have, that the ordinary Catholic is "just a lay person": in other words, someone who for some reason or another hasn't quite made the grade, who either isn't generous or bright enough

[1] Dorothy Dohen, a native of New York City, traces her interest in the lay apostolate to the vigorous liturgical life fostered among his people by the pastor of her home parish, the sermons he preached on the Mystical Body, her participation in a Catholic Action cell during her years at college, and other influences. In April, 1952, Miss Dohen became editor of *Integrity,* an important Catholic periodical "published by lay Catholics and devoted to the integration of religion and life for our times," and remained its editor until it ceased publication in June, 1956. She is the author of *Vocation to Love,* a book of spirituality for the laity, which has already been translated into five languages. Miss Dohen here presents a timely clarification of the concept of the lay apostle.

to be a priest or religious and therefore isn't expected to do very much or be very much in the Church; he can be content with being on the receiving end of priestly ministrations, can assume a passive role, and doesn't have to exert himself because as far as Christianity goes he is strictly an amateur. He is just a lay person!

Happily this area of confusion is being rapidly dispelled as the notion of Catholic Action—clarified, preached and encouraged by the Popes, particularly our last great Pontiffs Pius XI and XII—reaches more and more into the parochial precincts of the Church. But with the idea of a lay apostolate gaining popularity, another area of confusion has developed, often unfortunately aided by those who are most interested in the idea. This confusion arises from making a distinction between the ordinary man or woman (just a lay person!) and the Catholic who has chosen to "become a lay apostle."

I have been concerned for some time over this "professionalizing" of the lay apostolate, for a great many people, while admitting the fact of the lay apostolate, see it as a special vocation out of the context of normal lay life, a new exclusiveness meant only for the chosen few. They see apostolicity not as a mark of every Christian but as the trademark of a professional minority.

I first became aware of this distortion of the idea of the apostolate while I was editing *Integrity* magazine. I got a letter one day from a young man who wrote, "I wish I could be a lay apostle, but I want to get married and will have to support a family." (As if either marrying or earning a living were alien to being apostolic!) Then a doctor I know told me that she was warned by an anxious friend "not to join the lay apostolate" since, as the friend erroneously deduced, "it would mean giving up your practice."

This idea of the apostle as separated from the rest of men and lifted out of the society where men marry, work, and engage in temporal occupations is as false as it is dangerous. In this distortion, the Christian apostle called to penetrate every phase of society abandons the penetration to give time exclusively to "the apostolate"!

I hasten to add—in self-defense, since for over four years as editor of *Integrity* I was a member of the "professional" apostolate—that while normally the Christian exercises his apostolate in ordinary daily life and in ordinary "secular" occupations, there are some people who for the common good engage in some special task that needs to be done. But running a magazine, for example, is not the usual expression of the lay apostolate, although it may be the expression that attracts the most attention. However, the Christian lawyer, accountant, factory worker, typist, farmer, housewife, student, nurse, or chemist may be participating as fully (or even more so) in the apostolate of the Church.

The clarification of this idea of the lay apostolate has engaged my thoughts for a long time. While I see the danger —which I have outlined above—of the restricting of the name *apostle* to a chosen few, I also see a danger in making the notion of the lay apostolate so broad and vague that, while including everybody, it affects nobody. For, while the Christian becomes an apostle at his baptism, he has to exercise the faith that is in him, he has to make conscious effort to fulfill his apostolic function. He may do this in several ways: by becoming active in *Catholic Action* proper (which is the official participation of the laity in the apostolate of the hierarchy); or he can engage in the work of the various organizations that form the broad *apostolate of the laity;* or because of circumstances or his own particular talents he may choose to exercise his apostolic mission only by *being Christian* in *his own walk of life* and there doing his utmost to Christianize his environment. The point is that as a Christian he is an apostle, a witness, not primarily in what he *does,* but rather in what he *is.*

I think this latter distinction is of the greatest importance, for otherwise *apostolate* can become synonymous with *activity* (or even with *activism*) and the work of Christians, the plans they make, and the efforts they put forth, can become just like the activities of Marxists, Socialists, Republicans, Ladies' Aid-ers, or Elks. The true apostolic mission of the Christian can never be divorced from his personal growth in holiness.

That is why it is inevitable that considerations of spirituality for the laity and thinking on the nature of the lay apostolate should go together.

As I hope I have made clear by this time, the Christian *is* an apostle. Therefore, it would be rather misleading for me to say that through such and such a set of circumstances I decided to become a lay apostle. As a baptized, confirmed lay person I am necessarily a lay apostle. I had the good fortune, however, to be baptized and confirmed in a parish where the pastor took the apostolic role of the layman seriously. At the time, needless to say, I did not realize how fortunate I was. It wasn't until after I was grown up that I became aware how naive I had been to think that all pastors were like ours and gave sermons on the Mystical Body of Christ, encouraged participation in dialogue and high Masses, and told the school children that the only important thing in life was to become a saint. Our pastor's vocabulary may have been slightly different from the apostolic jargon we use today, but he put the same ideas across.

At college I was one of a group of girls who started a Catholic Action cell on campus, took reforming the world very seriously, acted with enthusiasm and often with imprudence, agitated for interracial justice and an integrated student body (when such things were still novelties even for Catholic colleges), and graduated with the conviction that the one thing necessary was to do God's will. Four of my friends did this by entering contemplative convents (which proves the self-evident truth that participation in the lay apostolate nurtures religious vocations). Amid all this extra-curricular activity at college I managed to learn enough English and philosophy to serve as an invaluable background for any writing I have ever done.

Contact with the Young Christian Workers, the Grail, and with the group who started *Integrity* magazine, greatly influenced my thinking. I began writing quite by accident, and because I agreed, on the whole, with the objectives of Ed Willock and Carol Jackson, the first editors of *Integrity,* the magazine became a convenient outlet for my articles. A group

of these articles, which attempted to formulate a spirituality
for lay people, have been collected in a book, *Vocation to
Love,* which was published by Sheed and Ward in the fall of
1950. This book has since been translated into French,
German, Spanish, Portuguese, and Italian—a circumstance
which, needless to say, made me very happy. For I have
benefited exceedingly from the various writings and activities
of lay people in Europe (who had, it would seem, a head start
of a generation or so in responding to the needs of the Church
for an ardent, informed laity), and I was delighted that my
book could be used as a small payment on this debt. Further-
more, these translations have made me conscious anew of the
unity of the universal Church—the consolation there is in
sharing the same problems, in working together to re-Chris-
tianize our troubled world.

   With the April, 1952, issue I assumed editorship of *Integrity*.
My predecessors, Carol Jackson and Ed Willock, had done a
magnificent job in awakening Catholics to the dangers of the
policy of giving an uneasy Sunday-lip-service-to-God-and-40-
hours-a-week-with-time-and-one-half-for-overtime-devotion-to-
Mammon. They realized, however, that "unenlightened heroism is not enough"; they therefore felt strongly that *Integrity*'s function was primarily an intellectual one; that its
aim must be to help form Christians who would not only have
"good will" but "good sense." They avoided, however, address-
ing themselves to scholars or specialists; rather they aimed the
magazine at *thinking* Christians—people who take a critical
interest in the modern world, who are awake to the crisis our
age is undergoing, but who are also alive to its opportunities:
in other words, people who would respond to *Integrity*'s aim
of working toward the new synthesis of religion and life for
our times.

   In the beginning *Integrity* was frankly iconoclastic—point-
ing out the false gods of the age who attract the unthinking
worship even of many Catholics. The editors did their work
with vigor and vision; they were revolutionary, but a revolution cannot last forever. When I became editor the magazine
entered a second stage, which I outlined in my first editorial.

"While we realize that we must clear away the rubble before we can rebuild, we know that 'rubble removal' cannot go on indefinitely. A certain amount of destructive work is necessary to make way for construction. But we feel there comes a time when we have an obligation to give plans for a constructive program, for a positive apostolate. . . .

"However, we do not claim infallibility. We realize that in the reform of the temporal order there must be a certain leeway, a certain amount of experiment. No one can have the sole, ultimate answer for the reform of each particular nook in society; for there are certain relative factors which must be taken into account. In this area it is easier to be dogmatic about what is wrong than about what would be right."

How successful this second stage of *Integrity* was I cannot judge. The magazine was forced to suspend publication, the last issue being that of June, 1956.

I hope that *Integrity* served its purpose in the apostolate of the Church; but, needless to say, an editor is too close to a publication to assess its value or influence. Personally, I am grateful for the opportunity of having edited *Integrity*. I know editing it did a great deal for my own intellectual development and maturity. But again, I am still too close to the experience to evaluate it accurately.

I can only hope for myself personally that I will grow in understanding of the dignity and responsibility of the Christian lay vocation. I hope, too, that I shall be allowed to share Teresa of Avila's simple, proud boast, "I am a daughter of the Church."

Who Hunger and Thirst after Justice

JAMES B. CAREY [1]

INASMUCH as my topic is my own reaction to a wide variety of "social action" programs, I will in the course of this article have to deal with the subject largely in personal terms. For that reason, I am impelled to apologize at the outset if I seem to violate the dictates of modesty.

I was graduated from high school in Glassboro, New Jersey, in June, 1929. More mature readers, in point of age, will recall the postwar era which was then referred to as the "Prosperous Twenties." It was a period marked by the advent of prohibition, of the teen-age flapper, of ruthless free enterprise, of an impoverished farm population, of stationary wage rates and steadily rising corporate profits, of wild speculation in corporation securities and of unlimited credit granted without consideration of ability to repay. More important were the advent of what the Kremlin rulers today call the cult of the individual, and a resurgent isolationism that made other countries and

[1] James B. Carey, a native of Glassboro, New Jersey, went to work in the Philco plant in Philadelphia shortly after graduating from high school in 1929. Within a few weeks America was suffering from the economic ills of the stock market crash of October of that year and the depression that followed. Seeking answers to the many questions in his own mind as well as in the minds of millions of others, Mr. Carey read widely on social problems. At length he was introduced to the great social encyclicals, that have since so profoundly influenced his thinking. His interest in labor and its problems led to his election as secretary of the Congress of Industrial Organizations at the age of twenty-seven. Today, Mr. Carey is President of the International Union of Electrical, Radio and Machine Workers, AFL-CIO and vice-president of the American Federation of Labor and Congress of Industrial Organizations.

continents seem as remote as the planet Mars. What concern was it of ours, the chosen people, that there was widespread unemployment in Britain, France, and Italy, a crushed Germany, a mysterious thing called communism at work in Russia? If these people had problems, said we, they were of their own making, and the solution was none of our concern. It could never happen here.

This incomplete list of descriptions occurs to me from the vantage point of 1956. Most certainly they could not be detected in 1929 by the callow 18-year-old high school graduate. At that time, like almost all of my 140,000,000 fellow American citizens, I was concerned only with me. For I had an ambition—a college degree in engineering. As one of eleven children in our family, I could not look to my hard-working father for financing. My plan was to seek a job—any job—save my money for a start in college, and get through by working part time. I opened my campaign.

If I had had any prior conditioning for thinking, it was that the wonderful thing called American mass production afforded me a target, and so I decided on production engineering as my field. I had little difficulty getting a job in the Philco plant in Philadelphia, and I registered for night courses at the Wharton School of Finance of the University of Pennsylvania. That was my status when the stock market crashed in October, 1929.

I admit here quite frankly that I felt little or no concern over what was happening in so remote a place as the New York Stock Exchange. In my thinking, people who owned corporate stocks were wealthy folks who could afford to take a loss. I didn't know that they had been gambling with money borrowed from the little savings bank accounts of little people like my father and our neighbors in Glassboro. I found that out when the little banks, and some big ones too, began closing in the Glassboros all over the country. I found it out also when dealers in Philco products began cancelling orders in large numbers. Above all, I found it out when on each weekend I saw large groups of much older and more skilled workers than myself plodding dejectedly from the plant clutching their final pay envelopes to join the laid-off hundreds and thousands who were streaming from other factories.

In this sad welter of confusion and despair I was as much mixed up as the overwhelming majority of my fellow citizens. All of us were constantly subjected to a barrage of explanations from prominent citizens that the situation was merely the working of mysterious things called "economic laws." And, we were told, economic laws were part of a general system of Natural Law. All of these vague explanations only deepened our bewilderment.

If we accept as true the old proverb that "misery makes strange bedfellows," we must go a step further and realize that misery also has its compensations: it drives men closer together and rugged individualism begins to fade. I most certainly found myself discussing affairs with my fellow-workers whom I had before considered remote from my own personal plans. My contributions to the discussions were virtually all questions, and the answers that emerged should be of interest. We were told, and told one another, that the answer lay in socialism, in communism, in syndicalism, in anarchy. There were of course an endless variety of suggested applications of each of these panaceas. Pamphlets of every variety appeared, some of them passed out at plant gates by men with the gleam of fanaticism in their eyes. I read them all. I went beyond the pamphlets. From public library books I learned of Saint-Simon, Owens, Marx, Engels, the Utopians, the Socialists, the Communists, and all the other radical splinter groups to which the writings and doctrines of the masters had given inspiration. I came out of this undirected, personal research with two conclusions: a) none seemed to have more than a part of the solution; b) each of them devoted a lot of time and space to denouncing all the others. It was at this point that chance, or more likely Divine Providence, brought me to a new point of departure.

One Saturday evening, journeying on a bus up to Glassboro to see the family, I found myself seated beside a Catholic priest. A conversation developed, and presently I found myself pouring out my problems, to which he listened with unbelievable patience. When I had run through what I now recognize as a weird composite of half-baked notions, he finally spoke.

"Have you in your investigations ever run across a publication called 'The Condition of the Working Class'?" he asked.

I assured him I had not. He then explained that Pope Leo XIII had written such a document back in May, 1891.

"You certainly ought to look at every aspect of the problem," he went on. "Get it and read it. You probably can buy it for a dime in a Catholic bookstore."

He wrote the Latin title, "Rerum Novarum," on a slip of paper and gave it to me. A few minutes later we parted at Glassboro where I alighted, without, alas, asking him his name. I have never met him again.

My upbringing had been in what is usually referred to as a "good Catholic" home. Our devout parents had seen to it that we learned the Baltimore Catechism by heart from cover to cover, that we attended Mass and other ceremonies regularly, that we approached the sacraments as required. But never, never, never had I been told that the Church had a social philosophy, that the Catholic Popes had written on the subject. It will therefore be easy to understand why I was only casually impressed by what my priest companion had told me on the bus. I did, however, take the trouble the following week to make the rounds of the Catholic bookstores in Philadelphia until I found one that had what I wanted. I sat down at the first opportunity to plod through "Rerum Novarum."

Anyone looking here for a repetition of the miraculous flash of light that blinded Paul and tumbled him from his horse as he journeyed with companions toward Damascus will look in vain. My first reading left me with a great deal of frustration. It seemed to me that the poverty and misery of 1891 were being used by Pope Leo to bolster the old catechetical teaching with which I thought I was familiar. I wanted a more direct solution, one that would immediately meet the needs of people. Little did I realize at the time the impression that my prior readings had made on my consciousness. I was in fact saturated with materialism.

I found in "Rerum Novarum," however, some observations

of the pontiff that appealed to me. First was the revelation that his denunciations of greedy and miserly employers equalled and in many cases outdid the radicals I had been reading. Secondly, Pope Leo quite clearly urged workers to organize into unions for their own protection. It was these two points that led me to read "Rerum Novarum" again. To my surprise I found other points that I had overlooked on my first reading. Subsequent readings in the weeks that followed brought a stream of new revelations.

I am not qualified to make or even attempt to make a philosophic analysis of "Rerum Novarum" or the two great social letters, "Quadragesimo Anno" and "Divini Redemptoris" that came from the pen of Pope Pius XI in the eight years that followed my "discovery" of "Rerum Novarum" during that dismal winter of 1929–1930. I will, however, assert that my subsequent rereadings of all of them brought to my attention ever new points. It therefore gives me only tragic amusement today to be told by anyone that "I have read the encyclicals and know what they say." I have probably reread those amazing letters every three months for the last twenty-five years, and I never fail to come up with things I have overlooked. I've quite given up trying to grasp it all. I am guided by papal social teachings because they present a down-to-earth, common-sense approach to the solution of human problems, an easily understood presentation of the eternal truths on which man's relationship to man and to his God must be based if a suffering world is to recover its sanity.

Back in 1929–1930, however, I knew much more about everything than I know now. What probably saved me from myself was the slow realization that moral and spiritual values must go hand in hand with the quest for man's material sufficiency. It was that important truth, I learned, that had been overlooked, ignored and even derided by the social philosophers I had been reading.

In my discussions with my fellow-workers I continued to meet with a wide variety of opinion. It was not the atmosphere in which to quote Leo XIII directly. It was, though, distinctly the time and place to discuss the principles he advanced. My theme therefore became the simple idea: justice.

Now and again I had heard older workers muttering that back in World War days they had had the protection of "the union" in such matters as wage rates, hours of work, seniority and other benefits. It was out of their muttered comments that recognition of the need for union organization began to emerge. Like others, I looked to existing labor organizations for help. It was not forthcoming. The organized labor movement was weak. During the twenties, hundreds of thousands of workers, deluded by the gleam and glitter of false prosperity, had dropped their union affiliation. Conscientious labor leaders had striven in vain against that trend. Other leaders had ignored it. It was a rude but healthy jolt for me when I realized that unions do not organize workers; they organize themselves and all an existing union can do is afford them an opportunity to do so. However it came about, my fellow-workers at Philco began to organize themselves.

I will not endeavor within the limits of this presentation to set forth in detail the progress made from that small beginning at Philco. It is sufficient to say that today the Philco Local is designated Local 101 of the International Union of Electrical, Radio and Machine Workers with 450,000 members in other local unions from coast to coast in the United States and Canada. The designation No. 101 indicates that the Philco Union in which I still hold membership was the first local chartered in the first district of the International. That small beginning at Philco spread to other plants in the Philadelphia area and thence to electronic manufacturing plants in other areas.

Neither will I go into detailed descriptions of how the Communists infiltrated our union. To all of us communism was a mysterious thing—a foreign animal which none of us knew. The issue at that stage was bread, and the Communists promised bread in abundance. None could challenge that material approach. It was therefore extremely difficult for me and those who agreed with me to hold the line on programs that would fit wholly within the framework of a truly democratic society in which decisions based on justice could be reached. The one advantage I had was a "party line" that was not subject to the changing whims of men.

Let me say with regret that in those early struggles the young industrial union labor movement had to fight its own battles. We received no help from employers or from our government. On the contrary, both employers and government officials on the whole bitterly opposed our efforts. In addition, we were part of a divided labor movement, a large segment of which still clung to the craft union type of organization that had stemmed from the individual handicraft industries of the eighteenth century.

When our union became affiliated with the then American Federation of Labor, I became in the course of time a general organizer for the AFL assigned to work in the electronic industry. That job brought me into the higher councils, and it was then that I discovered a hard core of responsible leaders who were committed to the organization of industrial unions in the great mass production industries. And that discovery brought me to a friendship with a man whose personality, intelligence and philosophy were to affect all the rest of my life.

That man was Philip Murray.

Some day, probably years from now, a biographer with a genius for analysis, interpretation and expression will write the life of Philip Murray. I would not attempt the job, although I do feel I have some competence as a witness.

Phil Murray as I knew him was a grave and quiet man. His patience and kindliness seemed illimitable. Never in my many years of friendship with him did I know him to resent a personal affront. But I also came to learn that there was armorplate steel beneath his usual forbearance. Let an aggressor make clear his malice toward the group, and one could see the gleam of the steel beneath the silk. But the offender would be treated with patience and kindness even then, and Mr. Murray would afford him ample opportunity to mend his ways. That point being passed without results, Mr. Murray would act with devastating effect.

I must confess myself as a naturally impatient man, and my impetuousness in those early days can well be imagined. I poured my problems into Mr. Murray's ear. Never once did he tell me what to do. Instead he proceeded deviously to lead me to form my own conclusion based entirely on principle. It can be seen that that was not an easy job when it is remembered that I was twenty-three years old when I first met him.

I knew from other sources that he was a devout Catholic, but some little time elapsed before it dawned on me that the basic principles he was expounding were neither more nor less than the principles set forth in the papal social encyclicals. He had never mentioned papal teaching to me, and so the revelation made a deep impression on me. I had been trying to reconcile what I had found with the events in which I was moving. Mr. Murray simply took the better way of trying to reconcile events to the principles set forth by the Popes. It was to take some time, however, for me to realize fully that Mr. Murray agreed with those principles because he recognized their accuracy and truth, not merely because the Popes had seen fit to write about them.

My organization, loose as it was in 1935, was in the group that withdrew from the old AFL as a result of the craft unionism vs. industrial unionism controversy. Not long thereafter many of the segments of organization in the electronics manufacturing field joined together and formed the United Electrical, Radio and Machine Workers, and I was elected president. The UE played an active part in the great campaign that culminated in the establishment of the Congress of Industrial Organizations as a constitutional body in 1938. It was then that I found myself, barely twenty-seven years old, elected as secretary, the second administrative officer in a national labor organization, the CIO. Our president was John L. Lewis, and Mr. Murray was elected vice-president.

Looking back, I now know that the days passed quickly to the fall of 1940, when Mr. Lewis gave up the presidency of the CIO and Mr. Murray was elected as his successor. It was just another brief period until Mr. Lewis and his United Mine Workers withdrew from the CIO, and I assumed the combined office of secretary and treasurer of the national organization.

Meanwhile, things had been happening in the UE. I knew, of course, that there had been communist elements in the union from the beginning. What I did not know was the long-range program to which the Communists were dedicated. I learned in 1941, however, when I suddenly found myself ousted from the presidency and saw the Communists take over complete control. The reader will understand the dismay with which I went to Mr. Murray only to find him calm and imperturbable as usual. I know I was angry and vindictive. He let me talk myself out, then he spoke.

"You know, Jimmy," he said, "that on a night just about 1900 years ago, a Man met with twelve men for supper in Jerusalem. As a result of that meeting, eleven of those men went forth, leaving the twelfth behind with his philosophy of materialism. The eleven went forth to organize the greatest movement for social good the world has ever seen. Even though they and their followers had to pass through flame, oppression and accept death itself for hundreds of years, they did organize it. Nothing worth having comes easily. Honest men do more than fight evil; they fight to replace evil with good."

I have never forgotten that crystal-clear summing up of encyclical teaching voiced by an extremely practical, humble man who had a vast knowledge of a practical world. He had taken that method to urge me to rally what discomfited supporters I still had in the UE and continue the fight. Mine was not the only CIO union that was dominated by the Communist Party. In my personal resentment I did not see at once, as Mr. Murray did, that the UE was only a part of the problem. Millions of other CIO members did not see it either, but their eyes were completely opened in 1949 when Mr. Murray, his patient efforts to effect reformation having finally run their course, coldly and dispassionately laid the problem before the annual CIO convention. At his suggestion the accused criminals were given a last chance to mend their ways. When they did not, the UE and ten other unions were expelled. I am happy to report that of the 800,000 individual members involved, more than 650,000 are now back in the legitimate labor movement, 450,000 of them in the International Union of Electrical, Radio and Machine Workers, AFL-CIO, of which I am presently the president. The shattered bastions of the Communists' once proud labor fortress are steadily crumbling, and I can see the day when the site will be a level plain.

We of the old CIO have been criticized, of course, for the "delay" in dealing with our communist groups. It should be remembered, however, that the free labor movement throughout the world did not invent communism or import it to the United States. Its formulas stemmed from its causes. In organizing the labor movement to its present strength, the CIO and the AFL had to take a calculated risk. Had we turned the early organizing campaigns into a war against communism, it would have well satisfied the large employers who so bitterly opposed the organization of unions. We had a larger target, and we still have it: organization of the un-organized—an objective solidly in consonance with papal social teaching.

As the Popes have pointed out, unions, like all other voluntary segments of society, must be free of domination by other economic, political or ideological groups. The best illustration of this is the situation with which the world was confronted during and immediately after World War II. I need not stress the fact that when the war ended in 1945 I was probably one of the most bitter foes of communism. Hence I was somewhat surprised when I was called into a highly secret meeting by Phil Murray and the late Sidney Hillman, president of the Amalgamated Clothing Workers, to find that they were giving serious consideration to an affiliation of the CIO with the proposed World Federation of Trade Unions. Earlier I would have opposed any such procedure, but experience had taught me to listen to them.

Their reasoning was that the labor movements of the war-shattered nations were as weak and tired as the nations in which they existed. They saw those unions as prime targets of

Soviet diplomacy, with the political company unions of Russia serving as the vehicle. They felt that we had an obligation to do what we could to rally the bona-fide unions of the world to resist the onslaught. We did just that, and I had the rare privilege in the four years that followed of serving as Mr. Murray's personal representative in many international labor conferences here at home and in many European cities. In my judgment, we were successful, although not completely so. History has already recorded that the subjection of the communist satellite nations began with Soviet subversion of the native labor movement. When we and the greatly strengthened unions of the free nations withdrew from the WFTU in 1949, we left behind us a hollow shell that the International Confederation of Free Trade Unions, which we and the AFL united to organize, has since rendered virtually impotent. I believe we of labor could have given some good advice to our diplomats.

The joint approach of AFL and CIO to the ICFTU was the first step in the campaign that culminated in December, 1955, when both groups met together in convention and merged into one organization. Along with Walter Reuther and David J. McDonald, I served as one of the three CIO officials that met over many months with George Meany, William F. Schnitzler and Harry C. Bates of the AFL to work out the details. One of our first agreements was that a labor organization must have more than a material objective: that it must also concern itself equally with the moral and spiritual values that are so important in an orderly society. Those concepts are clearly set forth in our AFL-CIO Constitution, and there are rigorous penalties, now being enforced, for their violation.

I am impelled at this point to clear up a widely-held misconception. Despite the left-wing labels that many employers, politicians and editorial writers try to pin on my colleague, Walter Reuther, I enjoy nothing more than to hear Mr. Reuther, a non-Catholic, presenting the current objectives of organized labor in terms of papal social teaching to a meeting of informed Catholic priests.

In conclusion, I want to express my gratitude to the many bishops and priests who have, despite our many shortcomings, encouraged and supported our efforts to bring about the reconstruction of the social order.

We Are the Revolution

ROMEO MAIONE [1]

PROBLEMS? Who's got problems? That was my feeling six years ago. After all I was making $62.00 a week. Of course, I was spending $62.50—my mother gave me the extra 50 cents for taxi fare to enable me to collect my check on Friday. But I had no problems, or so I thought.

I remember coming out of my house one night and a friend of mine saying, "Hey, Rom, where are you going?"

"Just to the hangout," I replied. "Hangout" wasn't the right word for it. I ought to have called it home. I knew the restaurant-keeper and the bartender better than I knew my own father. But that evening my friend talked me into going to the meeting downtown. The first person who greeted me at the door was a priest.

I nudged my friend and whispered to him: "Listen, what's the idea of bringing me to a religious meeting?"

Reluctantly, I sat down with six other young fellows, and the priest began: "Well, this is an open meeting, pick your discussion subject for the evening." He looked at me and

[1] Romeo Maione, the former president of the Young Christian Workers in Canada, has worked zealously and lectured widely on this movement in America. At present he is living in Rome, where he is associated with the Permanent Committee of International Congresses of the Lay Apostolate. He is also a member of the International Bureau of Young Christian Workers, which has its headquarters in Brussels. The address of YCW in Canada is 62A St. Mary Street, Toronto 5, Ontario; and in the United States 1700 W. Jackson Blvd., Chicago 12, Illinois.

asked, "Would you have a topic, a problem that we could discuss tonight?"

"Father," I answered, "I haven't any problems. I have a pretty good salary, a car, everything's pretty good."

The atomic bomb was hanging over our heads, but I had no problems.

"Fine!" the priest said. "We need a perfect person for this group; it will help the group out."

Finally we decided to discuss family life. We talked about the spirit at home, how members of the family got along with one another. I recall one question vividly, "When was the last time you went out with your father?"

When it was my turn to answer I hesitated, "I'm not sure— I suppose the last time was when he carried me out in his arms, quite a long time ago."

We discussed the importance of the family until one of the group exclaimed, "Gosh, this country is finished—among all the young workers I know, there is no real family life." The group decided on action.

"Jim, what can you do for this week?"

"Gee, I don't know."

"Well, how about staying home two nights?"

But Jim complained, "What am I going to do at home?"

"Well, stay at home two nights and find out what happens and report back next week."

Another fellow was to help out at home and report the reaction of his mother.

All I was to do was to go out with my father. Now that sounds simple. Just, "Go out with your father." But when you had not done it for sixteen or seventeen years, it was like going over Niagara Falls in a barrel. The meeting was on Tuesday. Wednesday night I thought I'd put it off until Thursday. Thursday I put it off again. Finally on Monday I got brave and asked my dad. I needed even more courage to pass my usual hangout. I kept wondering what the reaction of my pals would be. But this was a unique experience in my young life, and I shall never forget it. I had discovered that it was fun to go out with my father.

I relate my introduction to the Young Christian Workers because in that first meeting all the essentials of this revolutionary youth movement were present. Here was a practical program designed to meet the problems of youth. What are some of these problems?

In the minds of many the most pressing problem centers around the attitude of the modern world to the sixth and ninth commandments. It is true that there is an organized conspiracy to undermine Christian marriage by extolling divorce, birth control, and other perversions, and in a more subtle way to seduce the unalerted by the glorification of impurity through immodest books, dress, amusements, movies and any other means calculated to degrade man to the level of the new paganism. St. John Chrysostom pointed out, "It is impossible for anyone who leads an impure life not to grow weak in the Faith." And St. Thomas Aquinas adds, "The highest faculties of man, the intelligence and the will, are disturbed most of all by sins of impurity." And the enemies of Christ are well aware that when human beings become corrupt by impurity they will allow themselves to be enslaved by other evils without reaction.

As the foundations of the family were tottering, it could no longer carry out its function of imparting basic religious, social, and cultural formation to the child. As a consequence, he emerged as the lost youth and he was plunged into a working life where the positive denial of God's rights left no gauge to measure respect for man's rights. It followed that leisure time was necessarily directed to means of escape from such crushing reality.

Though this pagan attitude toward marriage and the family presented one of the serious problems facing Catholic youth, it was only one phase of the total situation that brought the YCW into being. Much more urgent were the economic and social conditions of the workers' world which had such devastating moral and spiritual implications.

Across Europe, even in Catholic countries, the worker had become a victim of the materialism of a modern industrial society which was indifferent to the startling truth that "raw material leaves the factory ennobled and transformed, while men are corrupted and degraded." Man had become a living tool, and was valued only for his part in the production of goods. As a result, the workers all too frequently were either drugged into apathy towards Christ's interests, or were revering as banners of redemption the satanical pennants brazenly unfurled by the Communists in all parts of the world. Besides, without equipment for the real struggle to live as members of Christ, they were succumbing to the pressure of His enemies, and many of them sought some solution to their miserable situation in that cloaked tyranny which posed as the friend and liberator of the working man.

Of course, this degradation of the worker's dignity has a long history. It began when he was deprived of the guilds, those vocational groups which reflected in the economic sphere the solidarity of the Mystical Body. The process was considerably accelerated by the deadening effects of the industrial revolution, which reduced the worker to the level of a machine. Thus robbed of his human dignity, the worker was left in a state of utter frustration and bewilderment, and his innate craving for justice and happiness had to be satisfied by whatever was within his reach. Now, his soul in a sort of torpor, he was lulled into believing he had no problems or at least that they didn't matter.

But they did matter to those priestly hearts touched by compassion for the unfortunate of every kind. It mattered so much that one of them, a Belgian priest, Canon Joseph Cardijn, appalled by the misery of it all, and stunned at his rejection by his former friends, factory workers, because he was now a Catholic priest, personally requested of Pope Pius XI permission to devote his life to the workers. It is hardly surprising that this great pontiff of Catholic Action gave his blessing and support to the young priest who seemed a providential answer to his own lament that "the greatest shame of the twentieth century is the loss of the working classes to the Church." Every year of his life afterwards, the Holy Father received this zealous priest in audience.

The devotion of Canon Cardijn materialized in that dy-

namic form of the lay apostolate, the Young Christian
Workers, which gained official recognition in 1925, and which
grew like the mustard seed from Belgium across Europe and
throughout the world until today it exists in 62 countries and
embraces two million workers. When the movement celebrated its silver jubilee in Brussels in 1950, 51 nations were
represented. In February, 1956, its international statutes were
approved by the Holy See.

This tremendous growth would seem positive proof that the
young Catholic worker cooperating with other young workers
for Christ's program is an answer to the need of our times. I
have devoted my life to its progress because I believe it is
God's will for me. A few years ago, while giving a talk in a
large Canadian seminary, I was asked by one of the students
what it was that really converted me to YCW. After a little
hesitation I replied, "When I realized that I was responsible
for finding a solution to the problems of youth, I could no
longer complain, 'Why doesn't the government do something
about it?'"

After I had been in the movement for some time, I made a
retreat under a YCW chaplain, and I have never forgotten
the theme of that retreat: "From the beginning God had you
in mind. He created you to do a job at a certain point in time.
He has given you the necessary talents to do it, and if you
fail, it will remain undone for eternity. Some special task is
given to every human being, and it is this thought that gives
meaning and purpose to life." It was in YCW that I learned
that everybody has a vocation, a special work for which he
was created. I now know that as it is the obligation of every
Christian to bring Christ into the everyday activity and leisure
of those around him, it is my special privilege and responsibility to bring Him also to the problems of modern youth
so that they themselves can solve them through Him.

Pope Pius XII, in speaking of the YCW, said: "What is
needed is the active presence in factories and work places of
pioneers who are fully conscious of their double vocation—as
Christians and workers—and who are bent on assuming their
responsibilities to the full, knowing neither peace nor rest

until they have transformed the environment of their lives to the demands of the Gospel. The Church, by this positive constructive work, will be able to extend her life-giving action to the millions of souls for whom she has a maternal and ardent solicitude."

This transformation of their environment by the workers is the aim of our great mass movement. Its program is to recruit and train young working men and women first to discover and then to meet their crucial problems in this workers' world; to develop work leaders for a better world tomorrow. Such a program involves education in every phase of spiritual, economic, intellectual, recreational, and social life—an education which will infuse in them the Christ-like spirit essential to the apostolic charity which is the soul of the movement, and fitting to their status as missionaries in the mission fields of their individual environment.

The technique adopted is that of the small group. Such a group of six or eight young workers meets regularly with a lay leader and a chaplain for intensive study and spiritual formation. Each member of this original group later forms another group or "team" by gathering together a number of other workers to discuss their problems and to undertake appropriate action. Thus the apostolic spirit generated in the small group is channeled through the teams to inspire and influence the workers of the world—even those not interested. For the Young Christian Workers are trained in the concept of the immeasurable worth of the individual soul. They know that Christ would die again, and that His Mother would stand again beneath the Cross, for the redemption of a single one of them. They are positive that Christ was meant to live in each worker's heart without exception, and they are convinced that the solution of the problems affecting the worker's temporal betterment should go hand in hand with his spiritual formation.

All the problems of his life are scanned by the worker, and all the pagan influences brought to the searchlight of truth which reveals their corruption. And not only his own problems concern him, but those of his neighbors, his fellow-

workers, his friends, and acquaintances. As a result of this
training in the development of personality and judgment, the
solution to a problem can often be arrived at by an individual
or the cooperative effort of a small number of workers; more
often the concerted thought of many is required. The YCW is
organized locally, nationally, and internationally, for while a
parish problem may be handled on the spot, another may
require government legislation.

It is not only big problems which invite probing into; it
is not only big achievements which are taken into account.
There is a spirit of service in the YCW which expends itself
in those little things which often make or mar individual
happiness. They might include helping a new neighbor get
acquainted, visiting a lonely shut-in, baby-sitting to enable a
young married couple to go out together, searching for suitable apartments, encouraging attendance at union meetings,
passing out literature—all the innumerable acts of supporting,
encouraging, and rendering directed by the spiritual and
corporal works of mercy. If much can be done, much is
expected; if only little can be done, nothing more is required.

The Young Christian Worker, unlike the Communist, is
acutely conscious of individual capacities and the varying
inequalities of human conditions and opportunities; consequently, haste is never expected in the development of the
worker. We have known the joy of seeing a man who never
read take an interest in the newspaper headlines or editorials,
and the delight of learning that a girl who never prayed now
offers a "Hail Mary." Or it may be that a worker consistently
indifferent to his neighbor's need begins to think about the
man down the street, the girl at the next desk, the couple
around the corner—discovering in their hopes his own, and
in the solutions to their problems the eliminating of his own.

Possibly the first change may be the internal one when a
man begins to notice the world and his fellow-men in the
reflected glow of God's love—marvelling at the goodness and
beauty of what he observes until his mind is lost in the
thought of the infinite perfection of the Mind that conceived,

ordered, and created all things, and made man to His own image and likeness.

Thus, without perceptible change in his activity or his perspective, the worker's development begins with his offering to God of the ordinary things of his everyday life. Our Divine Lord said that a cup of water given in His name would not be without its reward, and St. Theresa of the Child Jesus knew that picking up a pin for love of Him is recorded in eternity. It is when we see the "beginnings" that we are especially glad that our Patroness is the saint of small actions consecrated to God—as well as Patroness of the missions. And often the small actions in themselves grow big, like the Marriage Preparation Course.

It was evolved from a campaign undertaken by the YCW in Canada to ascertain the thoughts of the average youth on marriage. Week by week the staggering reports came in of how little was known about that vocation, the true notion of love, the necessity of financial preparation, the housing situation. Solutions were worked out, courses devised, ideas put into practice. One group, for instance, began a parish savings fund to help workers prepare for marriage. When all the information was gathered, when problems were faced and eliminated, the results were so striking that the Marriage Preparation Course of the University of Ottawa was born and is now reaching out to vast numbers of young workers across Canada and the United States. Other services directed to the workers of the world include YCW boarding houses, employment bureaus, parish libraries, low cost vacation cottages, retreats and days of recollection.

A chaplain is essential to the small group as the guide who moulds the young workers so that they will become accustomed to recognizing themselves as members of one Body engaged in the struggle for the reorganization of the world under Christ, the Head. He is sympathetic to the aspirations of the workers, and helps them to bring these aspirations into harmony with the interests of the Mystical Body. He presents the proper perspective, he upholds the ideal, inspires the vision, and is indispensable to the spiritual formation of the members, although, as a priest, he cannot be a member of the YCW, for it is a lay organization. He does not direct, he inspires; he does not give lectures, but listens and discusses the facts as discovered by the members.

Recently a YCW chaplain had this to say about his role in the formation of lay apostles: "There are many people who consider the lay apostolate as some sort of hobby with priests, not springing from their vocation to the priesthood. But from my own experience I can say that outside of offering the Mass and dispensing the Sacraments, the formation of lay apostles is the most important part of my work. It was not until I started a YCW group that I really understood what it meant to be called 'Father.'"

The ideal YCW chaplain is the priest who has learned from Christ the method He used to select His Apostles and the technique He used to bring them to the full dedication so needed today. Whenever the question is asked, "Why can't we develop leaders as zealous and dedicated as the Communists?" the YCW chaplains will reply, "Such future leaders for the cause of Christ are now being trained in our small groups and teams."

The regular meeting usually follows a general plan, opening with the young Christian Worker prayer:

Lord Jesus, I offer Thee this day all my works, my hopes and struggles, my joys and sorrows. Grant me and all my fellow-workers the grace to think like Thee, to work with Thee, and to live in Thee. Make me able to love Thee with all my heart and serve Thee with all my strength. Thy kingdom come in all our factories, workshops, offices, schools, and in all our homes. May those of us who may be in danger of sin remain in Thy grace, and may those who have died on labor's field of honor rest in peace.

Sacred Heart of Jesus sanctify the Young Christian Workers; Sacred Heart of Jesus, Thy Kingdom come through the Young Christian Workers.

A review of the previous week and a report on action accomplished come next, followed by a reading from one of the

Gospels and an application of some aspect of Our Lord's life to the worker's life.

The next phase of the meeting is the Social Inquiry session, the pivot upon which the training of the YCW swings. It is the kindergarten and the university of life in action—an educational device so effective that it has been adopted by almost every apostolic group in existence. After various attempts and experiments with other methods in his struggling groups of young workers, Canon Cardijn devised the system from the three steps outlined by St. Thomas Aquinas for arriving at a prudent action—Counsel, Judgment, and Command. For the workers the priest simplified this to See, Judge and Act.

The YCW apply this formula to each problem, so that the solution to it is based on Christian prudence after thoughtful deliberation on all its aspects. The very people involved, those concerned with the stark reality of everyday life, make the decisions which help them in the most practical and efficient manner. Thus the whole man is directed to the knowledge of Christianity and to the application of that knowledge to every condition of life—in short, this technique is the key to fulfilling our obligations as members of the Mystical Body to the common good and the development of our individual personality.

And so this new kind of revolution goes on, and the workers are grateful for the march of their army so far, but restless until they have recruited all the young workers of the world. To this end, at numberless tables of YCW groups, priests are painstakingly, patiently planning the campaign and briefing the officers on the strategy of restoring the divine order of God's plan in the working world; and trusting to achieve it through Mary, the Mother of God, the Queen of the Apostolate.

Catholicism on the Secular Campus

JEROME G. KERWIN [1]

To LIVE one's early years in a community part
Jewish and part Catholic has definite advantages. For the
rest of his life one has an immunity against the virulent
affliction of anti-Semitism and has treasured in his memory
examples of the exercise of charity. In the community of
which I speak, which was located in one of the older sections
of Albany, New York, lived second-generation German Jews
whose families came to this country in the 1840's to escape
social, political, and religious persecution; side by side with
them lived second-generation Irish whose forebears came to
the United States at about the same period and for similar
reasons. The memories of oppression were still vivid in the
minds of these people. They had learned to live side by side
in the New World in peace and good-neighborliness. We
Catholics came to know the kindness, the generosity, and the
helpfulness of the Jewish people, whatever turn life's fortunes
would take. All celebrated together bar mitzvah and confirmation, all rejoiced at weddings and anniversaries, and all grieved

---

[1] Jerome G. Kerwin, a native of Albany, New York, has been a member
of the faculty of the University of Chicago for thirty-three years. He has
contributed articles to Catholic and secular periodicals, and has written several
books. He has given generously of his time, talents, and energy to many
Catholic and public causes. Imporant as these activities are, perhaps Professor
Kerwin's greatest contribution to the Church has been the example of his
life as a Catholic, a scholar, and a teacher at the University of Chicago and the
fatherly interest and concern he has shown for the welfare of the Catholic
students on its campus.

at deaths and misfortune. This was the New World, freed of the rancors, bitterness, and hatreds of the Old.

Within the community was the public grade school, as cosmopolitan in makeup as the community itself except for the teaching staff, which was ninety per cent Catholic—as noble and God-fearing a group as was ever assembled under one roof. I can still remember vividly those teachers on holy days calling to their desks each Catholic child to inquire if he had attended Mass. A negative answer brought a stern order to leave and get to Mass at once and to report back promptly after having fulfilled his obligation. One looks back with profound respect at the work of those teachers of youth whose staunch Catholicity in no way prevented their meting out equal justice and charity to all under their charge.

When I was seven years old my family moved into a large house not far from the Cathedral. Living within the shadow of the Cathedral had its effect upon all daily living and activities. The impressive brownstone edifice with its high graceful spires dominated in many ways the life of a large area. The solemnizing of the great feasts with complete ceremonial brought home to each one of us the full meaning of the liturgical year. Naively, many of us youngsters could not believe that Holy Week, or Easter, or Pentecost, or Christmas could be properly observed without the presence of a bishop. Nor could we quite understand why good Catholics from other parishes knew nothing about the blessing of holy oils or of the moving chants of Tenebrae. Later I was to learn how unknown the latter service was among large masses of Catholics. Many years later I observed to my pleasant surprise how it came to be adopted as a regular part of Holy Week by numerous Protestant churches.

No one in the Albany diocese at this time was unaware of the presiding Ordinary, Bishop Burke or, as he always signed himself, Thomas Aloysius, Bishop of Albany. No more beloved prelate walked the earth. He was affectionately known as the "Little Bishop," and everyone in the neighborhood awaited his evening walk in pleasant summer weather. It resembled a parish visitation—stopping to chat here, to visit there, to inquire about the condition of the ill, or the new job of this person or the lack of a job of that person.

But before the evening walk could get under way, a reception committee of a score or more of noisy youngsters awaited his coming down the steps of his residence, their mission something more than greeting their spiritual father. On the corner stood the neighborhood ice cream parlor. This was the mecca of the youngsters. Surrounded by them, the Bishop led the way down the street and into the ice cream parlor, where each young admirer got his treat of an ice cream soda. Needless to say, as the years went by, additions to this peaceful band of young pirates were readily recruited; I, too, was a member.

It would be unfair, however, to give the impression that the yearning for the sweeter foods of life was the only thing that brought the children to their Bishop. Early every morning they gathered about the episcopal residence to greet him on his way to offer Mass. Chatting and laughing, they tagged across the street with him to the Cathedral door. Yes, Thomas Aloysius was in every way the people's bishop. To my own family, however, he was not only Ordinary of the diocese, but a close personal friend. My mother's people had known him as a young curate and, later, as pastor of their parish. He was a consultant on many important family matters.

For my high school course I was sent to the Albany Academy for Boys. While this school was thoroughly Christian in a Protestant way, it was a far cry from the Catholic way. It was the school of Albany's first families of Dutch and English descent and the school to which New York State's Governors had sent their sons for many generations. Founded back in the early days of Albany's history, the school still occupied its original building, a brownstone structure boasting a huge fireplace in each classroom, partition walls so thick that they seemed indestructible, broad, majestic staircases well-worn by the feet of many generations of students, and walls hung with oil paintings of the stern-visaged fathers of old Albany.

The plan of education was based on that of the English

schools; the principal was the headmaster, the teachers were masters, the classes were forms. The curriculum consisted of the fundamental subjects of English, Latin, Greek, history, mathematics, and the sciences; and the training was rigorous. By tradition the students were destined for the New England colleges or Princeton, and they were trained to meet the entrance requirements of these schools.

The headmaster, Joseph Warren, known to us students as "Pop" Warren, personified the spirit of the school. A product of a Presbyterian New England family, he appeared stern and severe but a kindlier, more paternal, more understanding soul never lived. With the students, his word was law.

The students of the school caught Pop's sense of honor with every breath. No monitors watched them during examinations, and no prefects haunted the halls and schoolyard to detect infractions of rules. Never since have I seen such a sense of responsibility borne by any group of a similar age. My first experience with the ways of the headmaster came when I had been in the school about two months. In the career of a teenager, among life's less pleasant duties are the frequent visits to the dentist. The custom had just set in in my day. My dental appointment on one particular day was set for one o'clock in the afternoon. This meant that I had to be excused early from school. Observing the rule firmly set in my public school days, I brought a note from my parents addressed to the headmaster asking for my early release to visit the dentist. I duly presented the note to Pop, who read it, slowly raised his head, smiled very gently, patted my head and said: "My boy, this note is unnecessary; your word is sufficient."

Pop took a special interest in me. Whether it was because I belonged to the ever so small community of Catholics at the school or whether it was because I represented a special species in not being a member of one of Albany's first families, I shall never know. But he never failed to show respect for and interest in my Catholicism. A religious man himself, he apparently respected the attachment of the Catholic to his faith. He would tell me that Catholics should especially prize the institution of the confessional, which Protestants unfortunately did not have, and that the name Catholic as signifying the universality of the Church was a thing that Protestants might envy. He liked what he called "the spirit of adoration" among Catholics and their praiseworthy familiarity with Our Lord. He hoped that I would aspire to the priesthood, the greatest of all callings. While it is not for us to judge the eternal fate of any man, I feel that Pop Warren, long since gone to his Maker, is enjoying that peace surpassing all our understanding.

With the completion of my work at the Albany Academy, I entered Dartmouth College. Here was another school of Protestant (Congregationalist) tradition. However, I was not in such a minority as a Catholic as I had been at the Academy. Catholic students contributed about one tenth of the enrollment of two thousand students.

Dartmouth College is one of America's older institutions of learning; founded under Congregationalist auspices in 1769, it is now non-sectarian. It would be impossible to categorize all the types of thinking one found on the Dartmouth campus. One could find strict moralistic Protestantism, or the cultural lag represented by nineteenth century Darwinism and agnosticism, or the noisy undogmatic dogmatism of flaming youth espousing all of Sigmund Freud and the popular iconoclasm of H. L. Mencken. Here and there among the students were small groups of cultists, about whom in their own estimation the world revolved, always working very hard at being critical, original, and esthetic, and succeeding only in appearing bored and in boring all others. The coming of World War I decimated the student body, but its short duration and its successful outcome did nothing to change the mode of thinking except to further the cause of Freudian psychology and the general idea of unending progress toward a world millennium.

Obviously this was not a Catholic atmosphere. The spiritual welfare of the Catholic students was cared for by a parish priest who had charge, not only of the local town parish, but an additional parish about six miles away. Religion was a matter for Sundays and for holy days for most students.

Among the faculty one found a number of excellent objec-

tive teachers who tried manfully in matters pertaining to the
Church to be fair and quite impartial. A few behaved as if
they had a special mission in life to undermine what they
called "the preconceived ideas" of students, which generally
meant their religious ideas. Some never made any reference
to religion—an attitude springing from complete indifference
to the supernatural. Perhaps it was better that they did not
speak. Here and there among the faculty one would find a
teacher to whom religion, and particularly the Catholic
religion, was something that had happened and was now
"with advancing intelligence and enlightenment" on the
way out.

Why did so many Catholics under these circumstances
remain steadfast in their faith? It is my opinion that the lives
of the Catholic as of the other students were compartmental-
ized. In one compartment were their classrooms and study
life; in another was their outside social life; in another their
home life; in still another their religious life. The marvelous
accomplishment of keeping these compartments quite distinct
and often contradictory was, I believe, more characteristic of
a confused period in time than of a general mode of living
for most people.

Before entering upon my own college career, I had a long and
fruitful conference with the devoted pastor of my own parish.
Whatever fears he felt about my losing the faith he concealed
and proceeded on the apparent assumption that I was one
who could be trusted. The very psychological effect of this
was to strengthen my own determination that I would be
worthy of the confidence shown. He proposed a plan of action
for what he said would be the lacunae in the education I was
to receive. I was not to jump to conclusions on any problem.
"Keep calm like a true scholar. You are out to get educated
and to pursue the truth. Your teachers through ignorance or
lack of understanding may sometimes distort that truth. Your
education also will be partial, lacking any religious instruction.
For these reasons you will have to take upon yourself a large
burden of self-education. Finally, don't neglect the sacraments." These were his final instructions. He offered to keep

in close touch with me by correspondence. He was an intelligent, well-read man; his collected letters to me comprised
a whole course in higher education. No professionally prepared teacher could have done better in providing bibliogra-
phies, source materials, and selected documents.

With such assistance I found myself in many classes and
conferences the voice of "the Catholic point of view." At times
I felt awed and frightened at this responsibility and even to
this day I hope and pray I did not make any egregious errors.
On matters Scriptural, I found that I was a better source of
information on the New Testament than my non-Catholic
fellow-students; on the Old Testament I was not so sure. Here
my knowledge was more apt to stem from the vivid pictures
in my Bible history textbook. Such solid Old Testament information as I possessed centered about the very gory battles
of God's Chosen People with their enemies.

In the midst of my college career, having determined upon
teaching as my vocation, I prepared to study at one of the
larger graduate schools. My choice was Columbia University
in New York City. In some significant ways the atmosphere
of the graduate school was quite different from that of the
undergraduate. While in no way was the atmosphere Catholic,
the scholars under whom one worked were more tentative in
their judgments of things Catholic and less inclined to express
their views in sweeping generalizations. Not long before my
going to Columbia some noteworthy conversions to the
Church had taken place among its faculty, including those of
the outstanding historians, Parker Moon and Carlton J. Hayes.
These conversions had no doubt the effect of impressing many
with the fact that the Catholic Church was not a dead issue
and was by no means unworthy of the respect of intelligent
people. Sitting at the feet of the great masters at Columbia
for two and a half years, I came to respect the devoted and
objective scholarship of these educated men.

A Catholic club existed at Columbia—without benefit of
clergy. The Ordinary of the New York archdiocese, Cardinal
Hayes, had not yet (along with many members of the hierarchy) been converted to the idea of Catholic clubs at secular

schools. The result was an unfortunate isolation of Catholic officialdom from the great centers of learning. Professor Hayes was the "unofficial chaplain" of the Catholic club. Its meetings were not frequent, and its activities were no more than one could have expected from an organization living under a kind of ecclesiastical displeasure.

I shall always be grateful to the Department of Political Science at Dartmouth College for having invited me back to the college as a young, very green teacher, without any previous experience, to assume an instructorship in 1921. The only Catholic—no doubt the first—on the faculty, I was treated with every courtesy and consideration. The fact that I was a Catholic disturbed no one. I felt from the start a fully-accepted member of the academic community of this old institution.

I met with nothing but encouragement from the College authorities in founding a Newman Club for the Catholic students—more encouragement, I am sorry to say, from the authorities than from many of the Catholic students. The Catholic students fell into one of four categories: the indifferent; the boys who felt that membership in a Catholic club was making too much of a show of their religion, setting them apart from their fellows; the graduates of Catholic high schools who felt that they already knew everything about their religion and needed no further help; finally, the sincere, helpful students who welcomed this enrichment of their own and the campus life. With some misgivings the local parish priest gave his approval. It should be remembered that this was still the period when many of the clergy believed that the founding of Newman Clubs at secular schools would draw Catholics away from the Catholic colleges. Those of us who felt that this would not be the case, and who felt in addition that the Church should not lose contact with the important centers of secular education, were somewhat suspect. The effort to establish the Newman Club met with indifferent success. My own conviction was that, however few the number of students who showed interest, a permanent organization should be built up on that few and they might act as the leaven on the great mass. But the students became discouraged because of

the small number willing to work in the enterprise, and the
parish priest himself felt that this was a forlorn cause.

After two very pleasant years at Dartmouth I accepted an
instructorship at the University of Chicago. Here I found
myself the lone Catholic on an eminent faculty of about eight
hundred and in an atmosphere that was as far from being
Catholic as any I had previously lived in. For the first time I
found myself associated with the crusading atheist and the
anti-Catholic who was very vocal in his opposition. The
attitude of by far the greater number of my new colleagues
was one of complete religious indifference. If I happened to be
a person apart among my colleagues, I found that in a different sense I was just as odd a phenomenon among my
fellow-Catholics in the city. While the University could boast
of some of the world's greatest scholars and generally enjoyed
the reputation of being one of the most productive institutions
of learning in America, to Catholics it was the devil's work-
shop, brewing atheism, communism, and all manner of subversion. The farther removed from the campus the Catholics
were, the more iniquitous the University appeared. While
there was much of the truth in the Catholic attitude, the
exaggeration of it appeared to this newcomer as frequently
ridiculous and always appalling. If this University were
recognized as a great center of learning in most circles, and
it was, it seemed to me that however iniquitous it appeared to
Catholics, it was a challenge to them to meet and not to
withdraw from.

I had these tasks: First, to convince my colleagues that
Catholics did not walk on all fours and could be respectable
members of an academic community; second, to do something
for the four or five hundred Catholic students at the University; third, to bring about *a rapprochement* between the
Catholic community and the University.

As to the first task, I can only say that my colleagues for
the most part have been considerate and understanding. There
still remains, however, among many the feeling that a Catholic
social scientist does all his work with Rome looking over his
shoulder and constantly on the alert to censor, condemn, or to

turn into propaganda all that he does. That feeling will only slowly be overcome when there are many good Catholic social scientists and when more extensive scholarly relationships are established with the secular schools on the part of Catholics.

Cardinal Mundelein would not give official permission for the establishing of a Newman Club. His very able and understanding Chancellor, the present Bishop Sheil, advised me that I ought to form an unofficial group of Catholic students. This advice was followed, and the group was called the Calvert Club after the founder of the colony of Maryland. Our efforts met with greater success here than at Dartmouth, owing to the devoted attention given to the work by resident priests who were working in various graduate fields of the University. Among them, special mention should be made of Father Harold Rigney, S.V.D., Father Vincent Flynn of St. Paul, and Father George H. Dunne, S.J., of Phoenix, Arizona.

The third task, that of bringing about better relations with the Catholic community, has not been without success. While some few Catholics still regard the University as one important step on the road to perdition, the greater number have come to look upon it as a front-rank institution of learning that is capable of producing Catholic as well as non-Catholic scholars.

The great change in Catholic thinking about the University came with the advent of Robert Maynard Hutchins and Mortimer Adler. Neither of these men was a Catholic, nor did they have any personal desire to act as missionaries for the Catholic faith, but their energetic espousal of Aristotelian-Thomistic philosophy and ideas derived therefrom made Catholicism respectable in the secular academic world and caused Catholics throughout the country to look upon Chicago as the new center of Catholic intellectual life. The effect of their energetic teaching and lecturing on campus threw the University into a revolution, the counterpart of which had never been known at any American university. The Catholics on the faculty and in the student body suddenly found their faith the center of University controversy. They were objects of suspicion or direct attack by the opponents of "the new order." Catholics were delighted that the fundamental philosophy of St. Thomas was getting the attention it deserved, but they were not quite sure of the wisdom of the method of attack used by enthusiastic Aristotelian-Thomists. The virtues of charity and humility did not figure sufficiently in the heat of the controversy to satisfy the cradle Catholics.

Nevertheless, Dr. Hutchins believed that he had caused an intellectual ferment similar to the intellectual action at the University of Paris in the thirteenth century. Students read avidly the original texts of Aristotle and St. Thomas; they argued philosophical problems in small informed groups with as much heat as students in other universities argued athletic affairs. The student newspaper raged at the non-Aristotelian, and non-Aristotelian professors replied vigorously to attacks in their lectures. In almost every class small groups of Aristotelians whose enthusiasm often outstripped their knowledge badgered non-Aristotelian instructors.

Out of it all came a number of young, devoted converts to the Church. Officially to the Chancery office the University of Chicago did not exist, but instruction had to be found for the new converts. Credit for the care of the catechumens during this crucial period must go to Father George Dunne, S.J., to the Dominicans at River Forest, and to the curates of the local parish. Most of the converts were of Jewish origin, definitely converts by way of the intellect, who willingly suffered great trials in espousing the Faith. Some of them have since entered the religious life, and after many years I know of no apostasy among them.

Their coming into the Church brought new life to the Catholic group: it put them on their mettle. The newcomers, as is often the case, found riches in the Faith which the older Catholics had either forgotten or passed over. Daily Mass and Communion became the regular order of life among the Catholics, application of the liturgy received a new impetus, and the great intellectual tradition of the Faith aroused a new fervor even beyond the confines of the University.

With the death of George Cardinal Mundelein, Archbishop Samuel Stritch of Milwaukee was appointed Ordinary of the archdiocese of Chicago. Before he took up his duties in Chicago, I went to see him in Milwaukee to ask whether some care could not be given to the Catholics on the University campus. He was most cordial and sympathetic. He promised that a Catholic chapel would be established and a chaplain appointed. On his coming the promise was fulfilled. Father Joseph Connerton was appointed chaplain, and he has performed the important function of his post quietly and effectively. Since the 1940's, over twenty students, upon finishing their academic work, have followed religious vocations; about a dozen at present are in seminaries.

A persistent feeling still exists among some Catholics that the University is a center of subversive activity. It is true that it runs true to the principle of great secular schools in its adherence to a great measure of academic freedom. But diversity of points of view does not mean irrevocable radicalism. No Communist or person of communist leanings teaches at the University. No student has ever graduated from the University as a worker for the communist cause. But if the communist charge has been unjustly spread abroad, it must be remembered that at one time people were warning parents not to send their children to the University of Chicago lest they become Catholics!

For over thirty years I have been associated with non-Catholic colleagues at secular schools. What can I say about the position of the Catholic teacher? Catholics are being accepted more and more among non-Catholic scholars. They are, however, still few. Strange as it may seem, the physical and biological sciences boast the greatest numbers. But in these fields opinion does not play the part it plays in the social sciences and the humanities. In these last-named fields non-Catholic scholars regard a Catholic as a person so bound by authority that freedom does not exist for him. Every time a bishop speaks on things forbidden, every time a new book is consigned to the Index, the Catholic must laboriously explain to his colleagues that he still remains a trustworthy scholar. However well the Catholic may do his job, some measure of suspicion always remains. Not infrequently he treads a lonely path—suspect by his fellow-Catholics in trying to bring a better understanding of non-Catholic schools and scholars to his own group, and suspect also by his non-Catholic friends as being too closely bound to his own. Despite all this the sincere Catholic scholar cherishes his role as a kind of mediator between those of his Faith and those outside. Nor can he in all conscience forget his obligation toward those of his own Faith among the students. In his desire that Catholics be pre-eminent among their fellow-students in their performance, he may be somewhat more severe with his Catholic students—but it is hoped not unjustly so.

In all that has happened at the University of Chicago in the resurgence of interest in things Catholic, particularly in the bringing of souls to the Faith, I have felt as one privileged by God's grace to witness portentous events. Others have accomplished the great work that has brought intellectual conviction, and still others have led the converted into the Church. I have been one of the household of the Faith who has performed the simpler task of welcoming newcomers at the portals or encouraging the doubting to stand firm within the precincts of the Church.

Out of the Depths

A.A. [1]

I AM an alcoholic. I am also a Catholic who has returned to the Church since sobering up with the help of God and Alcoholics Anonymous.

I have told my story, publicly, at many A.A. meetings to try to help other alcoholics and constantly to remind myself that I am an alcoholic first, last, and always. I can never take another drink again or I will end up drunk . . . and lose everything that is wonderful and good that has come to me during the past eight years of sobriety.

I am forty-eight years old. I was an only child of an Irish father and a German mother, both of whom I love very dearly. I grew into adolescence as a shy, selfish, spoiled and self-centered person who was completely egocentric—not a bad

---

[1] A.A. (an anonymous alcoholic) is a business man, an executive in a New York advertising agency. After graduating from a Catholic high school, he enrolled at a large secular college where he began to drink so heavily that he was expelled in his sophomore year, though he later succeeded in being reinstated and in receiving his degree. His drinking became progressively worse, and during a period of ten years he neglected the practice of his Faith except to attend Mass occasionally with his family. A.A. has been sober now for eight years. Thoroughly convinced of the part played by Alcoholics Anonymous in his rehabilitation, he works zealously to interest others in its program; realizing that by the grace of God he is what he is today, he attends Mass and receives Holy Communion daily and gives generously of his time and energy to the apostolic projects undertaken by the active men's sodality in his parish.

Anyone interested in obtaining information about Alcoholics Anonymous is invited to write to the headquarters of the organization at P.O. Box 459, Grand Central Annex, New York 17, N.Y.

boy in the beginning, but heading for trouble as life began to unfold.

Having attended a parochial grammar school and a Jesuit high school, I was well indoctrinated in Catholicism. As a boy I once had dreams of becoming a priest. When I was twelve years old I was confirmed and took a pledge not to touch alcoholic beverages until I became twenty-one. However, when I was seventeen which was during the Prohibition era, I found that all of my high school friends were drinking liquor at parties and dances. At first I refused to drink because I was conscious of the pledge I had taken at confirmation. But I soon rationalized that as a teen-ager I shouldn't be held responsible for a promise that I had been forced to take when I was just a child. So I took my first drink at eighteen with a sort of resentment against the Church, and I had a sub-conscious feeling of guilt every time I took a drink after that, although I do not now blame this "forced pledge" for my eventual alcoholism.

The following year I went to one of the foremost Ivy League colleges in the East, and here it was that I began to drink in earnest.

I found that by taking a few drinks I could lose my self-consciousness. The first one produced a warm glow inside me; the second relieved my tensions, scruples, embarrassment and shyness. After the third drink, I began to lose my inferiority complex and could hold my head up high and talk to the other people I was with. After the fourth, fifth, and sixth drinks, I became bold, aggressive, smiling, confident, superior, and quite a ladies' man, or so I thought.

For the next twenty-two years I drank constantly, except for brief spells of going "on the wagon" during Lent or to get over some very bad hangovers.

During my second year in college I found that my drinking had become more important than my studies. I began to go around with a fast, high-stepping group and was delighted when I was elected to one of the heaviest-drinking fraternities on the campus. I was living less than a city block from the Catholic church, but I began missing Mass regularly because it was often too difficult to get up on Sunday after a hard drinking bout on Saturday night. I cut too many classes, didn't study enough, and failed my examinations miserably. The Dean told my father, as he expelled me, that I had "sophomoritis." What he really meant was that I drank too much.

Next I got a job in New York, went to night school, and applied for re-admission to repeat my sophomore year. I was determined, with grim alcoholic resentment, to get my diploma and then tear it up in front of the Dean to show him that I didn't care. I didn't know it at that time, but I realize now that this was the beginning of my irrational, alcoholic thinking.

Returning to college, I practiced "controlled" drinking and tried not to let it interfere too much with my work.

I never quite went through with my original threat, but after I had passed all my final examinations in my senior year, I notified the Dean that I wouldn't show up for graduation but that he could mail the diploma, which I still possess.

I started to work in the advertising business and began to develop the philosophy, "When you work, work hard and when you play, play hard." I began to do rather well in business and started to make a good-sized salary and bonuses. But by now I was drinking more and more, and the hangovers were getting worse and worse. My religion had become less and less important, and I went to church only when I felt like it and to the sacraments only once a year—because I had to.

By now all kinds of horrible things were starting to happen to me—blackouts (loss of memory) and pass-outs (loss of consciousness); loss of wallets and watches; waking up in the morning and not knowing where I had been, what I had done or where I had left my car the night before. Then I had a bad automobile accident. There was a big excavation on upper Madison Avenue in New York City which had three or four red lanterns on it to warn people. But I ran a speeding car smack into it. The result was two broken front teeth which were snapped off as the steering wheel struck against my mouth. The car itself was folded up like an accordion. But for the grace of God I might have killed myself, or worse, might have run into another car and killed some innocent mother and father with their children.

About this time I met a lovely Catholic girl and we were married. I never will forget her alarm when I got drunk and passed out at our engagement party. Her friends and her mother warned her not to marry a "no-good" who drank too much. I had started to become an alcoholic, although I didn't know it at the time.

My wife induced me to start going to Mass again, and this was not too difficult because we moved to the suburbs after our first child was born. But at the time the third child was born, I really had a field day. My wife was in a hospital in New York. I would leave her after dinner and stay out drinking and running around all night, just getting back to the suburbs in time to change my clothes, shower and go back to New York to work. Yes, my drinking was accelerating now in geometric progression.

I used to think that the only person who was hurt by my excessive drinking was myself. But I know now that I hurt my wife, children, parents, friends, clients, bosses, business associates and nearly everyone with whom I came into contact.

One night I came home drunk and when my son tried to reason with me and asked me to go to bed, I hit him in the mouth and chipped off part of his front tooth. I'll never forget the expression on his small face when his drunken father did this to him.

Three times I was arrested and locked up for the night: once in Boston for getting into a fight in a Chinese restaurant in Roxbury; once in Philadelphia for kicking through a plate glass door; once in Houston for being drunk and disorderly. But none of these danger signals seemed to teach me that I was not a normal drinker. In Houston, I got out of jail the following morning just in time to get back to my hotel, shower, shave and, with the aid of a couple of drinks, make a one hour speech at a sales convention. If I hadn't been able to do this, I would undoubtedly have lost my job.

I was getting along quite well in business by now, in spite

of the drinking escapades, and I suppose a certain degree of luck was still with me. I was in charge of a two-million-dollar account at the advertising agency where I worked. Once I went to the client's office, which was out of town, and spent a whole week there carefully going over the coming year's campaign with the advertising manager, the merchandising manager, the sales manager, the general manager and the president. Magazine four-color layouts, newspaper ads, motion picture films, radio recordings, and so forth, were submitted. Each of the client's executives had approved, but had made certain important changes in each of the ads. As a result, I had a whole notebook of all the changes that had to be made.

I left there and took the train back to New York and, of course, I started to drink to celebrate getting approval on a whole year's work. But don't think I went home to my family when I got back to New York. Not at all. I kept right on drinking and celebrating.

The next thing I knew I was lying on a door stoop as the cold grey morning dawn woke me up. My face was cut, and my wallet, watch, suitcase, briefcase were all missing. I grew panicky.

I went to a hotel, took a shower, bought a clean shirt, had my suit pressed and went to the police station to report my loss. The sergeant told me that some honest cab driver might have turned my property in to the Lost and Found Department. That is exactly what happened, and everything was returned to me.

I could have replaced all the layouts, radio recordings, and other advertising material because we had duplicate records and photostats of everything at my office, but I could never have replaced the notebook with all the changes suggested by the client.

I realized that if I had lost this material I would have been fired, and the agency I worked for would have lost this valuable two-million-dollar account. But this didn't happen. Again, it seems that it just wasn't God's will for this to happen at this time.

Strange as it may appear, I didn't miss too much time from

the office due to drinking—maybe six days a year, days like the Fourth of July and the day after Labor Day. Somehow, I could usually get myself to the office with the help of a few drinks.

We were still living in the suburbs, and my drinking was getting progressively worse and worse. I would go to the Commodore Bar every evening and consistently miss my train. Sometimes I would stagger home at ten, eleven or twelve o'clock at night with no dinner. About half the time I didn't want to go home and frequently stayed in a hotel in New York. Sometimes I wouldn't get home at all for a whole week.

By now, my good wife was really disgusted with my conduct. We saw priests. I took pledges not to drink. I fully and sincerely meant to keep these pledges, but I was an alcoholic and I had an incurable disease. However, I didn't realize this at the time.

My wife finally decided to get a separation. She consulted a lawyer who drew up separation papers, and I had to move out of our house and into a cheap New York hotel, where I lived alone for four months.

Finally I went "on the wagon" again and persuaded my wife that I would mend my ways and stop drinking; this I sincerely wanted to do. So we decided to move back to the city, thinking that the geographic change might effect a cure . . . but it never does.

Soon I was back to my old ways again.

By now I had literally been out of the Catholic Church for nearly ten years. Oh, I went to Mass on Sunday occasionally with the children, but what I mean is that I hadn't gone to confession or received Holy Communion for a decade.

Then one Monday morning I woke up with the "grand-daddy" of all hangovers. I simply couldn't get up and go to work. My wife called a friend of mine who had been in A.A. for two years, and he came to see me about 10:30 that morning. He put his smiling face into my bedroom and asked me whether I wanted a drink. I certainly did! I knew I couldn't get my wife to give me one, but my friend poured out a large glassful, handed it to me, and started to talk about A.A. Then he gave me another drink and left me a copy of the "Big Book," *Alcoholics Anonymous,* to read. I agreed to do this.

I read the whole book through that day and night, taking a drink after every few chapters. I promised to go to an A.A. meeting on my fortieth birthday and said to myself, "Maybe there just might be something to this idea that 'life begins at forty,' and maybe A.A. might be able to help me."

I went to the meeting and was very much surprised at what I found. Here was a large group of people assembled in a room. They weren't Bowery bums but well-dressed, soft-spoken, clean-looking, bright-eyed men and women who extended a helping hand to a fellow alcoholic. They talked to me about themselves and told me of their own drinking experiences and how they had found A.A., sobriety, peace of mind and a new way of life. They talked my language and they offered to help me.

After three months of this, I felt wonderful. I was sober, I looked much better and I was temporarily out of all my troubles with my wife, my children and my boss. But I still had some reservations about *really* being an alcoholic. Was I *really* an alcoholic or could I control it this time?

I looked back over my past life and rationalized that I had never been hospitalized, lost my job, lost my family, or any of the other things that eventually happen if alcoholics keep drinking. True, I had come pretty close, but I hadn't really lost anything, had I?

Was I really and truly alcoholic? Suppose I just drank light wines and beer? Suppose I drank only on week-ends and not during the week?

So I took that first drink that A.A. says is *the one* that an alcoholic should not take. At first I didn't get drunk. But eventually I did. I kept up this so-called "controlled drinking" for three months while still going to A.A. meetings and going to Mass on Sundays . . . occasionally.

Finally, I went away for three weeks' vacation, and now I was drinking very hard again. I was completely away from the office, from A.A. and from the Church. On the Sunday night that I was scheduled to return to New York from vacation, I started on one of the worst drinking bouts of my career. This time I couldn't stop by myself. Each morning I would wake up with my clothes and shoes still on, alone in my New York apartment, because my wife and children were away in the country. Then I would go out to the corner tavern at 8 A.M. and get two quick drinks. Then to another bar for another two drinks and on to a different bar for more drinks. By 9 o'clock I would feel better, but then I would get a bottle of whisky and go back to the apartment to drink myself into an unconscious stupor. My front teeth got broken off again, my face was all cut up, and I looked as if I had been through a meat grinder.

Finally, after ten days of this, I called A.A. and really begged for help. The great experiment of "controlled drinking" was at an end. I now realized that alcoholism is an insidiously progressive disease, which never gets better, but only worse.

I still hadn't lost my family, my job, or all my money. What I had completely lost was my self-respect. I found myself helpless and my life completely unmanageable, due to drinking. I felt that if I kept drinking I would end up dead, on the Bowery, or in a mental hospital. With this realization I surrendered to A.A.—completely this time and without any reservations whatsoever. This time I wanted sobriety voluntarily and for *my own sake,* not to please my wife or my boss as I had done the first time my wife contacted A.A. My sponsor told me that I should go to an A.A. meeting every night in the week now because my family was away and this would help to keep me out of bars. He also told me that A.A. would not only help me to stay away from the first drink, which is the one that starts up the compulsion and the craving for another, but that A.A. is a twenty-four hour program . . . one day at a time.

Then he told me that there are Twelve Suggested Steps that really make the program work. These Twelve Suggested Steps are:

Step One: We admitted we were powerless over alcohol . . . that our lives had become unmanageable.

Step Two: Came to believe that a Power greater than ourselves could restore us to sanity.

Step Three: Made a decision to turn our will and our lives over to the care of God *as we understood Him.*

Step Four: Made a searching and fearless moral inventory of ourselves.

Step Five: Admitted to God, to ourselves, and to another human being the exact nature of our wrongs.

Step Six: Were entirely ready to have God remove all these defects of character.

Step Seven: Humbly asked Him to remove our shortcomings.

Step Eight: Made a list of all persons we had harmed and became willing to make amends to them all.

Step Nine: Made direct amends to such people wherever possible, except when to do so would injure them or others.

Step Ten: Continued to take personal inventory and when we were wrong promptly admitted it.

Step Eleven: Sought through prayer and meditation to improve our conscious contact with God *as we understood Him,* praying only for knowledge of His will for us and the power to carry that out.

Step Twelve: Having had a spiritual awakening as the result of these Steps, we tried to carry this message to alcoholics, and to practice these principles in all our affairs.

The Twelve Steps constitute a new way of life for the alcoholic. The Second Step refers to a Higher Power which is thereafter referred to as God, as we understand Him. Alcohol is mentioned only once.

The whole program, I was told, is spiritual. "Easy does it," "First things first," "Live and let live," "But for the grace of God," are slogans which describe the A.A. philosophy . . . one day at a time.

By now I realized that I wanted my sobriety *at any cost* and dedicated myself to doing whatever A.A. told me to do. This was a germ of the humility that my sponsor said was the right basis to build on.

I further realized that there was something else I should do spiritually, for I was a Catholic.

I started to go to the church every morning and to say my daily prayers there, asking God's forgiveness for the many sins of my life and asking Him each morning to help me not to take a drink that day. Then when I came home at night from the A.A. meeting, I would thank Him for keeping me sober that day.

After three months of sobriety I agreed to give my first A.A. talk and wondered what I could possibly say that might help others. I found the answer immediately after the meeting. Several new people came up to speak with me and said that they had benefited more from what I had said than from remarks by people who had been sober for several years. This was because I was only three months away from the last drink and had a closer bond with the newcomer than the old-timers had. Of course, the speakers who had been sober longer had a far more important message that helped many others in the audience.

Before preparing my talk I sat down one night with a pencil and a large pad of paper and started to work on Step Four—the taking of a searching and fearless moral inventory. On one side of the page I wrote down my many, many sins of commission and omission during my twenty-two years of drinking. On the other side of the ledger, I wrote down the good qualities with which God had endowed me. Of course the bad habits far overshadowed my God-given good qualities. My course of action in A.A. must necessarily consist of trying to *accentuate the positive* and *eliminate* (one at a time) *the negative.*

This led me a little later to a general confession and a determination to go to daily Mass and Holy Communion to ask God to help me in my effort to become a better member of A.A., of the Catholic Church, and of the human race. This meant going back to kindergarten and relearning many facts about my religion that I had been taught years ago in school but had long since forgotten.

What happened at the end of my first year of sobriety, I'll never forget. I led an anniversary meeting at my own group. Two of my speakers were men who had been most helpful in getting me started on my way back to regaining my sobriety and opening the door to this wonderful new way of life. The third speaker was a man whom I had called on in his most desperate drinking hour and had been privileged to work with as he regained his own sobriety for a four-month period. Afterwards, my wife invited everybody back to the house where she served up a birthday cake with one significant candle on it . . . marking my first anniversary milestone of sobriety in A.A.

Then I attended my first A.A. retreat with the Matt Talbot Group. Eighty per cent of the men who attended this were Catholic alcoholics, the other twenty per cent being non-Catholics who were searching for some spiritual improvement and hoping that perhaps the Catholic Church might provide what they were seeking.

All during this time I was attending meetings regularly, speaking whenever I was asked to do so, and trying, by Twelfth Step work, to help other alcoholics who asked A.A. for help.

I was making new friends—real friends—all over the city and in the suburbs. I was attending meetings whenever I went out of town on business. Today in most cities there is a telephone number listed under A.A. or Alcoholics Anonymous in the local telephone directory. When I arrived in Baltimore on business one day, I called up A.A. headquarters there. They told me that a group from Philadelphia was speaking that night in a large auditorium. When I got there I introduced myself as a New York member, and I was asked to substitute for one of the scheduled speakers who had been taken ill. Although I didn't know anyone in Baltimore at the beginning of the meeting, I felt that after speaking to that group I had made two hundred new friends . . . all people who had the same alcoholic problem as myself. After the meeting, an attractive couple drove me back to my hotel and I had breakfast the next morning with a visitor from Chicago who, like myself, had attended the Baltimore meeting to keep in close contact with A.A. while he was away from home.

About this time I learned that my parish was reactivating a

sodality which had been discontinued for twenty-five years. So three Catholic A.A.'s and myself were among a group of twenty-five men who decided to join in this form of Catholic Action and thereby try to get closer to God.

I have been an active sodality member now for four years. I realize that this has been a means of learning more and more about the Church and helping as a lay apostle in various ways suggested by the sodality. It was a real privilege to serve as perfect of this sodality for one year.

I have been sober in A.A. for eight years now, one day at a time, and I can truly say that I have never been happier in my life. Materially and financially God has blessed me with a wonderful job in the upper income bracket, but far more important is that I like and enjoy my work and the people with whom I do business. And I have learned something about prayer. In the past, my only prayers were to ask God for something material or beneficial to me and my family. Now I know that the thing I earnestly ask God to do is to show me what *His will is for me* and then to give me the strength and courage to carry it out, regardless of the consequences. I have learned that there is nothing so bad that can possibly happen to me that one drink won't make it a thousand times worse.

It may seem strange for me to say so, but I have even learned to thank God that I am an alcoholic, for my alcoholism led me to A.A., which opened my eyes to life in general, and specifically to what I could do to try to lead a fuller, richer life as a member of A.A., a Catholic, a husband, a father, a son, and a business associate. As Bishop Sheen has so eloquently said, "There could be no Easter Sunday unless there had first been a Good Friday." Every alcoholic that I know has had his own kind of Good Friday, and those who are sober and happy today in A.A. have truly found the joys of Easter.

A.A. has led me back to God *as I understand Him*. Without it I might still be leading the same old drinking, sinful life. But for the past eight years I have been going to daily Mass and Holy Communion in an effort to know God better and to ask Him to help me not to take a drink for twenty-four hours. With the assistance of God's grace and the A.A. program I hope to continue going straight down the line of sobriety, one day at a time, for the rest of my life.

By Way of Calvary

MARY ELLEN KELLY [1]

"MARY ELLEN, *I just don't see how you can lie there, year after year. It's certainly a good thing God didn't want me to be an invalid, because I simply couldn't take it."*

The first time I heard this I was tempted to retort, "That's what *you* think! You might not like it, but you'd take it, all right, because there wouldn't be anything you could do about it!"

It was not until quite some time later that I made a discovery: when health is snatched away or the free movement of one's limbs forever stilled, there *is* something one can do about it.

This delay was understandable, for though the pain of rheumatoid arthritis infiltrated my body before my eighth birthday, I was too preoccupied with ways of camouflaging its crippling effects to bother analyzing them. Even when this strange disease evicted me from the enchanted world inhabited by sixteen-year-olds, I did not—dared not—look beyond the

[1] Mary Ellen Kelly was born in Marcus, Iowa, where she still lives. During her childhood she contracted arthritis, and by the time she had reached her sixteenth year the painful ailment had confined her to her bed. She could easily have withdrawn within herself and become a victim of dejection, hopelessness, and self-pity. But her strong faith and her devotion to the Blessed Mother, aided by a suggestion from a Jesuit priest, led her to found the League of Shut-In Sodalists and to edit its bi-monthly paper, *Seconds Sanctified.* In directing the League and in editing *Seconds Sanctified,* Miss Kelly has found a unique apostolate for herself and has immeasurably enriched the lives of hundreds of shut-ins throughout the world.

moment then existing, and, after a sufficient number of moments had accumulated to make a day, I looked back only long enough to ask God to forgive me for those I had not borne patiently, and to accept the rest.

The need for pretense ended abruptly in the fall of 1939, when, in an impersonal hospital room miles from my home, I acknowledged the fact that I had become a totally dependent invalid—unable to walk, sit upright, turn my head, or use my hands. There was indeed no need for concealment now. The presence of illness could scarcely be more obvious.

In the months that followed I grew accustomed to my new world; but whether this adjustment emanated more from prayerful resignation than from a quiet certitude that escape from this unpleasant planet was highly improbable, I do not know. With pain making jealous demands on my attention, I seldom had either the opportunity or the desire to search my heart for motives.

But as the inflammation in my joints started making a reluctant retreat, I became curiously aware that despite the suffering which God was permitting me to endure, He had spared me from thinking that He had made a dreadful mistake or was being cruelly unjust. Tears often found their way to my collar, and occasionally the suspicion arose that my Heavenly Father was deaf; yet it simply did not occur to me to question His right to do with me as He willed.

Knowing just what it was that God's will entailed for me was another matter. That I carry a physical cross was His "expressed" will, a priest explained. The rest of His plan, he added, would be revealed in His own good time. Although I believed this, it was difficult not to wonder if the time would ever come. A year passed, then another, and still another, with none of them showing any indication that God had anything special in mind for me to do except offer to Him my continued inactivity, frequent operations and the embarrassment and annoyances created by my loss of physical independence.

As 1943 reached the last day of its tour, Father James L. McShane, S.J., the nurses' retreat-master, stopped in my hospital room for a chat. Though unsuspected by me at the time, this meeting—like the four years that preceded it—was a part of the groundwork necessary for the special assignment which was soon to be disclosed.

"Have you been a patient here long?" the young Jesuit inquired after introducing himself.

"Since 1939, Father."

His reaction to this made me like him immediately, for instead of shaking his head sadly and murmuring "tsk, tsk," he simply grinned and remarked, "Oh, a newcomer."

In keeping with the holiday spirit, our conversation skipped merrily along, heading nowhere in particular but enjoying the trip. Suddenly it took a dangerous turn when the blackrobe asked, "Are you a member of the Sodality of Our Lady?"

"No, Father, I'm not. And incidentally, that's a rather sore spot with me."

Encouraged by his interest, I explained that I had been unable to become a sodalist while in high school because no sodality was established in our school or parish at that time, and that later, after my hospital sojourn began, I had watched with longing as the nurses observed Sodality Sunday and made preparations for their monthly meeting. As the desire to become a sodalist grew, my sense of being left out, of wanting to know the joy of *belonging,* had also increased.

"It's a shame," I concluded, "that no one has ever started a sodality for shut-ins exclusively!"

Regarding me for a long moment, my visitor finally spoke. "I agree. Why don't *you* do something about it?"

In the fifteen months that followed, I often wondered why in the world I had accepted that priest's challenge. My plan had been favorably received by Father Daniel Lord, S.J., and other noted sodality leaders at the national headquarters in St. Louis, Missouri. But because of certain questions it raised, and in an effort to judge my staying power, *The Queen's Work* staff took its time to decide on it. Thanks to Our Lady and my Irish ancestry, each delay only served to magnify my determination to see the project through. It also served another purpose. In the summer of 1945 I left the hospital and returned home for good. After five years spent in an atmosphere of excitement, the relative silence and inactivity of my home town created in me a disturbing sense of restlessness that lingered in spite of my gladness in being with my loving parents on a full-time basis. Fortunately for me, they understood my eagerness to promote an apostolate for the sick and encouraged me in my efforts.

Under Father McShane's guidance, four other invalid girls joined me in the important task of defining the aims of our organization. These aims were as follows:

> To unite the sick, aged, and disabled in prayer and suffering for the honor and glory of God, the sanctification of their own souls and the salvation of the souls of others. To foster in our members an ardent devotion to the Blessed Mother and to attain through the help of her Sodality a more intimate union with Christ Crucified. To show our members the value, need and power of illness or disability.

These were the Seven Promises each member was asked to make:

1. To be resigned to God's will in sickness and in health.

2. To consecrate one's sufferings and disappointments daily to Our Lady in union with, in reparation for, and in loving honor of the Passion and Death of her Son.

3. To set aside one day each month in special honor to Our Lady of Fatima, our Patroness.

4. To spend fifteen minutes a day in mental prayer, and as much time or more in spiritual reading; to say a Hail Mary for *The Queen's Work* staff.

5. To say a Rosary each week for world peace and the conversion of Russia.

6. To recite daily the prayer of St. Francis of Assisi.

7. To dedicate four Sundays of the month as follows: SICK SUNDAY: For the sick and dying, especially for sick sodalists; MISSION SUNDAY: For those laboring in mission fields and for all priests, especially

those who remember us in their daily Mass; HOLY
FATHER SUNDAY: For the personal and general
intentions of Pope Pius XII, our fellow sodalist; ALL
SOULS SUNDAY: For the souls in Purgatory, weak
converts, prisoners, the persecuted, and fallen-away
Catholics.

Then, at my request, His Excellency, Most Reverend
Edmund Heelan, Bishop of the Sioux City diocese, appointed
as the League's spiritual director Reverend T. J. Schulte, S.J.,
of Denver, Colorado. This jovial priest fully qualified for this
role, for he possessed not only an unusual capacity for kindness, but also a deep understanding of suffering, having under-
gone the amputation of both legs.

Finally, my stubbornness had paid off. On April 13, 1945,
with Bishop Heelan's approval and blessing, the League of
Shut-In Sodalists opened for business—the business of helping
the sick. During the same eventful week thrity-five copies of
our bi-monthly publication, *Seconds Sanctified,* were mime-
ographed by a neighboring Lutheran minister and mailed to
prospective (I hoped) customers. Though I did not know
where the next postage stamp was coming from, it caused no
undue concern. The League had been dedicated to Our Lady
of Fatima, and I told her that if she would take care of the
finances, I would do the work.

I did not realize the measure in which this apostolate had
become integrated into my life until sixteen months later
when, through the initial efforts of Father McShane, a
pilgrimage to the major shrines of Canada was made possible
for me. In the midst of excited preparations, a sudden fear left
me panic-stricken: *If God should cure me, what would become
of the League?* Neither the thought of the long trip nor the
complications of making it on a stretcher worried me; but
haunting me day and night were the conflicting desire to be
well again and the realization that a cure would disqualify me
from the very organization which I had founded solely for
people like myself. The mere thought of this eventuality
plunged me into a pool of inescapable loneliness.

In spite of earnest prayers that I accept without question

whatever outcome should result, I felt distressed and confused at being pulled in two directions at once. Then the pilgrimage materialized, and all too swiftly it came to an end.

As the bells in the Basilica of Ste. Anne de Beaupré rang out in farewell, it became strangely clear to me that my not being cured was no mere accident. Now for the first time I was aware that my work with the League was undoubtedly one of the reasons why God had chosen me to walk the Way of the Cross, and why He did not wish to change the route.

With each year our membership has grown, and it is with deep gratification that the charter members and I watch our shut-in family increase both in number and in resignation to the ills that have befallen them. While striving to publicize our apostolate, we find that in our repeated references to its purpose and benefits, our own attitude toward suffering has assumed a more profound and comprehensive understanding. So are we constantly inspired by the heroism revealed in letters received from many of the members. In fact, their enthusiasm and zest for living provide us with an unending incentive to acquaint as many other shut-ins as possible with our League so that they too may benefit by their association as well as by the strength which is found in unity.

In 1948, a surprising boost in enrollment occurred after an article concerning our apostolate appeared in *The Catholic Digest*. From the German edition alone we received fourteen enrollment requests from Germany, including two in the Russian zone.

The charter members have contributed substantially to the development of the organization. Arthritics Madonna Fox, Mary Veronica Kelley and Dixie MacMaster have made it known throughout their respective areas (Rhode Island, South Dakota and Montreal) and, despite a severe spastic condition, Betty O'Brien of New Jersey has recruited dozens of candidates for our wheelchair brigade.

For three major reasons, the next two years were most eventful. First came the appointment of Monsignor William Boyd as the successor to Father Schulte, who had died the previous year. Our new spiritual director had been crippled

with arthritis for twenty years and was a resident patient in
St. John's Hospital, Rapid City, South Dakota. His example
and guidance have been of inestimable worth.

Next was the League's fifth anniversary, a happy occasion
highlighted by heartwarming messages of congratulations
from Boston's Archbishop Richard J. Cushing and Catherine
de Hueck Doherty of Canada. The League of Shut-In Sodalists was growing up.

The third cause of jubilation was an announcement that
made a dream come true. At an international meeting of
sodality directors in Rome, my original hope was realized
when the decision was made to permit the instruction and
reception of sodalist candidates by mail—a decision which
changed a 400-year-old precedent!

Now, for the first time, severely disabled and chronically
ill men and women who had been unable to belong to the
sodality could share in its blessings, for such barriers as remote
areas, the inability to attend church or school (where sodalities
are usually established), or a reluctance to be seen in public,
were removed. Those who had lived behind these barriers
considered this new ruling a personal liberation. Almost
immediately the Sodality for the Sick was established at St.
John's Hospital, with Monsignor Boyd as director. Since then,
nearly four hundred shut-ins have completed their probation
period and been received as sodalists.

The results of all this? Part of the answer lies in the following membership report, which was sent to *The Queen's Work*
on January 10, 1956: Members in the United States—1562; in
foreign countries—356; deceased members—368. Countries
represented on our mailing list: Alaska, Argentina, Arabia,
Australia, Brazil, the British West Indies, Canada, England,
France, Germany, Hawaii, Holland, India, Ireland, Japan,
Malta, Mexico, Nigeria, Nyasaland, Pakistan, Panama, Para-
guay, Philippines, Puerto Rico, Scotland, Spain, South Africa
and West Africa.

As for other results, I am happy to say that most of the
adverse ones concern my job of editing *Seconds Sanctified*.
These, in my opinion, ought to be compiled into a book

entitled *Why Editors Turn Gray*. Though most of them were
not of earth-shaking consequence, one can readily imagine my
frustration upon finding (after hours of proofreading) either
the wrong name under a member's picture, an upside-down
middle page, the incorrect date line, a "continued-on-page-five"
article that was not, or such classical misprints as *Esther
Martindale, S.J., We wish to grate our new members,* or *It is
well for each of us to develop our spiritual lice* . . .

Occasionally I incur wrath by sending a time-for-renewal
notice to someone whose envelope, containing his renewal, is
at that very moment lying unopened in my mail kit. It has
also been my misfortune to overlook an incorrect address in
our "Birthday Preview," thus nullifying the victim's chances
of receiving congratulatory messages from his or her fellow
shut-ins.

That "his or her" reference recalls an error which caused
me a crimson glow. One of the League's most loyal supporters
asked me to enroll a young correspondent of hers from Spain.
The name was Angel Sole. When I introduced Angel in
Seconds Sanctified's "Who's New" department, I referred to
our new member as "she." Soon afterward, a letter from
Spain pointed out that I had classified among the fairer sex a
spirited and very masculine 21-year-old boy! Blunders like
that make me grateful that those involved are usually blessed
with a sense of humor.

The ability to laugh, to live with pain, to make the most
of faculties and movement impaired by disease or injury—
these are but a few of the qualities which I have observed in
the League's shut-ins. Not all of them have developed these
qualities, but we have yet to enroll an applicant in whom they
did not exist at least potentially. However, whether they are
well adjusted or not, none is exempt from the need of frequent
reminders that Our Lady is standing by, eager to support and
comfort, and that it is better to carry one's cross than to drag it.

Articles appearing in *Seconds Sanctified* serve this purpose
exceedingly well because, with few exceptions, they are written
by men and women who are intimately acquainted with the
chilling grip of fear and discouragement. This authorship

understandably prevents the afflicted from thinking: *"It's easy for this writer to advocate resignation, for what does he know about suffering?"* These contributors *do* know about prolonged illness and its constant limitations, for they too are following the route to Calvary.

Another effective feature designed to help the cross-bearer on his journey is "Who's New," a column in which newly enrolled members are introduced. Their brief case histories make a deep impression upon the readers because, for many of them, this is their first association with other invalids. They begin to experience the feeling of satisfaction that comes with the discovery of friends who truly understand and are similarly handicapped. Soon they are comparing their problems with those of other members and, to their surprise, find that they are not so heavily burdened as they once imagined. A subsequent sense of purpose and peace is virtually inevitable.

A spastic, for instance, reads of a helpless patient in a county hospital, and he gives thanks that he can walk—even though his step is halting. . . . An aged woman, confined to bed after a full and active life, reads how a young paraplegic mother manages her home from a wheelchair, and she resolves to stop complaining. . . . From an item about a leprous couple who had to give up their first-born, a tuberculous teen-ager receives encouragement to face a long separation from his parents.

Another source of inspiration is "Random Reapings," an informal feature reporting on the members' trials and triumphs. Motivated by the example of others, the new additions to our handicapped family begin to make scapulars and rosaries, collect Catholic literature and stamps for overseas missions, contribute to CARE packages for needy foreign members, and engage in the fruitful apostolate of the pen. Some of our group have made amazing personal accomplishments, such as those who have become professional writers. These are but a few of the advantages to be gained from a pooling of mutual interests.

There are, however, a small minority who, unfortunately, decline to take part in these activities because they believe that God is unjustly punishing them. Consequently, they are bitter, confused, unhappy, restless and bored. Perhaps even worse, they are convinced that suffering is a tragic waste and that they are leading a futile existence. In our efforts to show them that this attitude leads only to misery, we point out, by way of contrast, rather than by preaching, the error of their thinking. Our success is by no means assured, yet if letters are any indication, the compassionate Comforter of the Afflicted prevents our efforts from being put forth in vain, as is indicated by this message from Florencio Decayo, a World War II veteran now in a Philippine Islands sanatorium:

> I wish to thank you and your generous associates for all the spiritual charity you have accorded me, and for all the religious leaflets and issues of *Seconds Sanctified* which continue to come to me. I am sure that Our Lady will reward you, for she is now the treasurer of whatever spiritual earnings I have and ever will have. In fact, that is the essence of our sodality—that is, in its unity of prayer and suffering, we are truly sharing in the "communion of saints."

Because of modern trends which recommend the pursuit of physical comfort at any cost, human suffering has been branded as an outlaw—a sadistic, despicable villain that ravages the young and old alike for no reason other than to destroy. It is small wonder, therefore, that there are those who would condemn this alleged renegade without trial, and even go so far as to assist in his execution.

It is imperative that these trends be refuted by men and women who remember that Christ elevated suffering to a lofty height by choosing it as the means of redemption. Who would be more logical for this task than those who, like Our Lord, are born in the shadow of the Cross?

This, then, is the assignment of the League of Shut-In Sodalists. This is the message we must carry to the world if its sick and afflicted inhabitants are to fulfill their obligation as members of the Mystical Body of Christ. We must serve as white corpuscles, as it were, standing ever ready to rush to the wounds caused by sin and heal them with patiently-borne pain and suffering; then try to erase the scars through frequent applications of love and allegiance. But just as it is necessary that a wound heal from underneath, so is it essential that we cleanse *ourselves* before we can hope to apply our healing powers effectively to an outward source.

This simple fact imposes on me an obligation which is difficult to meet in moments when immobility ceases to be an accepted reality and becomes a frightening nightmare. But after frenzy has expended itself and frustration ebbs, I am calmed and reassured by the touch of Our Lady's hand on my heart. And as her fingers gently quell its erratic beating, I feel it swell with a kind of bittersweetness which enables me to appraise my assignment as a victim soul, remember that there is no love without sacrifice, and reaffirm my belief that "if thou carry the cross willingly, it will carry thee and bring thee to thy desired end, namely, to that place where there will be an end of suffering, though here there will be no end."

Making a Convert

FLOYD ANDERSON [1]

What makes a convert? What is it that happens
to change a man's religion, his deepest beliefs, and cause him
to adopt another religion? Often it is a simple thing; sometimes it is complex and long-drawn-out; but always it is the
product of much thought and prayer.

Sometimes only a nudge is needed to bring one face to face
with the realization that the Catholic Faith is the one true
faith; some truth always dimly realized but never brought
into the full light of one's mind. I think that sometimes that
happens with those who read the fine series of Catholic advertisements sponsored by the Knights of Columbus. Men or
women of good will read the advertisements as they appear;
and then all of a sudden they realize these are things they too
believe, though they may never have put them into words.
Then they begin to think, and then they begin to study, and
then to pray.

They do not always become converts; but at the very least
they have a better understanding of the Catholic Church, a
more complete realization of what it means, what it stands

[1] Floyd Anderson, a convert to Catholicism, traces the beginnings of his
conversion back to 1932. Having left his native state of Wisconsin, he went to
New York City and accepted a position as secretary to Father Wilfrid Parsons,
S.J., then editor of *America*. The splendid example of the Jesuit Fathers led
to his ever-deepening interest in the Church, and he was baptized in June,
1936. Today Mr. Anderson is managing editor of *The Advocate*, Newark,
New Jersey.

for, Who originated it. And that is a tremendous gain for the Church, and for our land.

And then, sometimes, the finger of God touches them; and He gives them the grace to believe; and they accept His grace and they do believe.

But, in the usual and ordinary course of events, there are preliminary steps and actions before they are receptive enough to accept God's grace. Let me give you a case history—my own.

Looking back over the more than twenty years that I have been a Catholic, it seems hard to realize when I was not. And yet I know that it was in June of 1936 that Father Gerard Donnelly, S.J., one of the associate editors of *America,* the national Jesuit weekly review, baptized me.

How did this come about? How did a native of Wisconsin, of Scandinavian descent, with almost no Catholic contacts for most of his life, with no interest in the Catholic Church, almost suddenly become interested?

Several answers may be given, and several were given, at various times during the past twenty years—but I'm not sure they were always the right ones, or that they were more than partially right in some instances.

There was the brash woman who bluntly said to my wife, "Did he turn Catholic to 'get' you?" And converts who have Catholic wives often get that type question thrown at them, either openly or by implication.

Then there was the one-time friend and co-worker who asked the inevitable "Why?" and I replied simply, "Because it is the one true Church." Perhaps that wasn't the complete answer, though it was a part of it.

Then there was the time I talked before the Knights of Columbus Council in my home town in Wisconsin, on the reasons why I had become a Catholic. The reasons I gave were the social encyclicals of the Popes; and again it was partly the right answer, the reason, but it was only partly the true story.

Where does the story of a conversion begin? It seems to me that it is a lifelong story—it is not just when one finally realizes the existence, the importance, the necessity of the Catholic Church that one's conversion starts.

I still remember my first contact with the Catholic Church. As a very small child I had gone to a Norwegian Lutheran church; my mother was Norwegian, and as often happens, she was the churchgoing member of the family, at least in my younger years.

Then we moved to another part of the city. My cousin went to the Methodist church—and so did I. It was there I was baptized, when I was eight or nine. Very likely I had been baptized in the Norwegian Lutheran church too, but I didn't know, and the Methodist minister wasn't taking any chances.

About that time I had a Catholic friend, and he invited me to go to Mass with him one Sunday. I didn't mind; but I remember nothing at all of the Mass. What I do remember is that we sat in the balcony of the St. Louis Church, a French church, and that either I or both of us—and most likely it was I because I didn't realize what was going on—caused some disturbance. And I still remember that a sister came over to us; and that we sat quietly after that.

That was the first time I was in a Catholic church—and the last time, for almost twenty years.

We had Catholic friends, of course; but we didn't think of them as Catholics—just as friends. They were close friends of our family; and as young people we used to go to the parish dances in St. Louis school hall. I still remember them—they were held upstairs, and Father Lefebvre, the jolly and chubby French priest, was always there, making sure that everyone had a good time.

The next "almost" contact with the Catholic Church was when a good friend and I decided we were not quite sure the Swedish Lutheran church we attended was the "true" Church. I don't know what decided our actions, but we started going to different churches on Sundays—the Presbyterian, the Episcopalian, and so forth, to see which we liked "best." We had the Catholic church on our list—down near the bottom— and we never did get there.

But one thing did happen during that period that made a

strong impression on me—and perhaps it was a sign of things to come.

At one of the meetings of the young people's group at our Lutheran church, the pastor—who was an excellent man of great knowledge—was talking about the Lutheran communion. He remarked that "our friends down the street"—meaning the Catholics in St. Louis Church—believed that the Body and Blood of Christ was received in their Holy Communion. I thought at the time, "But that's what it says in the Bible, that Christ said this is My Body and this is My Blood." The thought came into my mind, and I have never forgotten the incident—but it went no further.

The impetus to conversion came in 1932, when I went to New York to study. I had visions of being a financial and economic expert, and of course New York was the place to go. And I went.

But the year 1932, for those whose memories don't go back that far, was one of many economic difficulties; and I met them, too.

As my money ran out, I got a job with a trade publishing house, intending to go to school evenings.

Then, by one of those very curious and unexplainable circumstances, Frank Y. McLaughlin, a friend of my father, came to New York. I had never met him; he was an engineer and had been out of the United States for many years, in Mexico, Spain and many other countries.

But, again because of the depression, engineering jobs were scarce, and he had come back to our home town. There he renewed his acquaintance with my father; and before he left for New York he promised to look me up.

He did; and we became friends. I was a secretary, and I did some work for him at his hotel. He had other friends, too, and one of them was Father Wilfrid Parsons, S.J., then editor of *America*.

Another happenstance: Father Parsons needed a secretary—and Mr. McLaughlin recommended me for the job. And I got it.

I spent the next four years in the editorial office of *America*, before I decided to return to Wisconsin. They were the most productive years of my life—because during them I became a Catholic.

I think I can look back now and properly evaluate the reasons, where I couldn't have done so then. There were intellectual reasons, because before I became a Catholic I was convinced of the truth of the Catholic Church. But above all, there was the grace of God.

But before these, the ground had to be prepared, to be ready for the sowing of the seed of grace and of intellectual belief.

Picture the situation: there was I, a Protestant, unfamiliar with the Catholic Church, spending the hours from 9 to 5, five days a week, in the company of Catholic priests. I had to learn from scratch; I still remember someone 'phoning a simple question about Mass, and I said, "Just a minute. I'll ask someone." There was shocked unbelief in the reply: "Don't you *know*?"

And I am sure there were other incidents that, happily, I was unaware of, or that I have forgotten, where I may have embarrassed the Jesuit Fathers by my lack of knowledge, my gross unfamiliarity with things Catholic.

But I never knew it from them.

At that time, the best that could have been said about Catholicism and me was that I wasn't antagonistic; I held none of the libelous prejudices against the Church. Probably I was just a mental blank as far as the Church was concerned.

I had four years with the Jesuits; proofreading articles for *America,* checking page proofs; and I began to absorb an understanding of Catholic doctrine, a realization of the meaning of the Church's teachings applied to everyday life. It made an impression. I have often thought that those four years were better for me than if I had spent them in any Catholic college.

I learned more than just the application of Catholic teachings; five days a week I worked and lived with those who carried those principles out in their daily lives, in the things they did as well as the things they said.

It was bound to make an impression; and I often think that

the first favorable impression a non-Catholic receives of the Church is the example of a Catholic living a wholly Catholic life. There was—and it hardly needs to be said—no attempt to persuade me to become a Catholic. Looking back, it seems to me that the priests at *America* almost leaned backward to avoid giving that impression.

The time came when I wanted to learn more about the Catholic Church; I was becoming interested in it as a personal thing. I began asking questions. They answered them; but again, with caution, with a fine respect for my Protestantism. They answered the questions, fully and completely—but they never attempted to push the door open wider. The initiative was always left to me; they would tell me what I wanted to know, but they were very careful not to go beyond my questions.

But I still wanted to know more about the Church, the reasons for it; and I asked Father Donnelly for more and more information. I wouldn't want to say that he was reluctant, because he wasn't; but looking back it seems that I almost had to persuade him to give me the information I wanted. I'm sure he wanted the initiative to come from me. Finally we set up a schedule of instructions or conferences. Every noon for several months we talked about the Church; and, again looking back, it seems to me that I got a pretty complete course in theology.

Then there was a blank in my thinking. I felt convinced that the Catholic Church was the one true Church. I had no doubt at all in my mind, but I couldn't bring myself to take the final step, to become a Catholic. I still don't know why, after these twenty years of being a Catholic; but when I decided to leave *America*'s office and go back to Wisconsin, I suddenly realized that I couldn't go without becoming a Catholic. I had a real fear that if I left *America*'s friendly office without taking that step, I might never become a Catholic. And I didn't want that.

And so, one bright sunshiny day in June, 1936, Father Donnelly baptized me in the Jesuit church of St. Ignatius Loyola, on Park Avenue in New York City.

What made me a convert? First, of course, it was the grace of God, without which nothing could have happened.

But secondly, it was the example of the priests and brothers at Campion House, where *America*'s editorial office is. It was the living of the Catholic Faith by these Jesuits that made the first impression on me; their constancy day after day in that living that prepared the way for the sowing of the seed. Without that example, I wonder whether mentally and psychologically I would have been receptive to God's grace. Often I doubt it; though I have no way of knowing. But I think there is a point in this for all of us. All Catholics have it in them to be convert-makers—merely by the power of their example. God has given us a standard to hold high—the beliefs of our faith. We are witnesses to them before men; and as we are true witnesses, good witnesses, faithful witnesses, we have an influence for good on those we meet.

Whether we like it or not, whether we want to or not, we do carry with us everywhere we go the example of being Catholics. We are judged, not only as individuals, but also as Catholics. If we are true Catholics, we are shining examples. We bring credit to the Church; we put in the minds of others the thought that if these Catholics are good people, then the Catholic Church is a good Church. Contrariwise, if we are not good Catholics, we bring discredit, not only to ourselves but to the Church as well. We cannot avoid that.

When we are bad Catholics, again we are judged, not as individuals, but as representatives of the Catholic Church. We bring shame, not only to ourselves, but to the Church which we represent.

What makes converts? You do, and you and you and you; and I hope that I may too. We make converts, we bring people to a more receptive attitude toward the Church and its teachings, as we exemplify those teachings in our lives.

We help prepare the way for God's grace; and, God willing, we may even be the channels for God's grace, as He opens the hearts and souls of our non-Catholic friends to the glories of His Church.

We all profess the faith; we must all live it, too.

Apostolate to the Worker

DOROTHY DAY [1]

I WENT to the national shrine at the Catholic University on the feast of the Immaculate Conception. There I offered up a special prayer, a prayer which came with tears and with anguish, that some way would open up for me to use what talents I possessed for my fellow workers, for the poor.

As I knelt there, I realized that after three years of Catholicism my only contact with active Catholics had been through articles I had written for one of the Catholic magazines. Those contacts had been brief, casual. I still did not know personally one Catholic layman.

And when I returned to New York, I found Peter Maurin— Peter the French peasant, whose spirit and ideas will dominate the rest of my life.

When I walked into my apartment, I found waiting for me a short, stocky man in his mid-fifties. This man introduced himself briefly: "I am Peter Maurin. George Shuster, editor of *The Commonweal,* told me to look you up. Also a red-headed Irish Communist in Union Square told me to see you. He says we think alike."

[1] Dorothy Day, journalist and pioneer lay apostle to the workers and the poor, carries on her apostolate from 223 Chrystie Street, New York, N.Y. During the early part of her life she sought in vain for a cause worthy of her talents; and her search led to her conversion to Catholicism and her collaboration with Peter Maurin in founding the Catholic Worker Movement.

I remember several things about that first meeting, characteristics of Peter that were to impress themselves more and more on me during the years that followed. He spoke in terms of ideas, and he stressed the importance of theory. As people gathered around us in the movement which sprang up, this attribute stood out. He thought in terms of our common humanity, of our life here today. He stressed the need of building a new society within the shell of the old, "a society in which it is easier for people to be good." He wanted them to stretch out their arms to their brothers, because he knew that the surest way to find God, to find the good, was through one's brothers. Peter wanted this striving to result in a better physical life in which all men would be able to fulfill themselves, develop their capacities for love and worship. He wanted them to be able to produce what was needed in the way of homes, food, clothing, so that there were enough of these necessities for everyone. A synthesis of "cult, culture and cultivation," he called it, as he tried to give me the long view, the vision.

Peter made you feel a sense of his mission as soon as you met him. He aroused in you a sense of your own capacities for work, for accomplishment. He made you feel that you and all men had great and generous hearts with which to love God. If you once recognized this fact in yourself you would expect to find it in others. "The art of human contacts," Peter called it. But it was seeing Christ in others, loving the Christ you saw in others. Greater than this, it was having faith in the Christ in others without being able to see Him.

Although Peter came to me with sheaves of writing in every pocket which he either read aloud, or pressed upon me to read and study, he had not begun to write till late in life. All his writing, even his letters to me, were in phrased sentences, broken up to look like free verse. He liked to consider himself a troubadour of Christ, singing solutions to the world's ills, insinuating them into men's ears with catchy phrases.

When he read the articles I had written in *America, The Commonweal,* and *The Sign,* he was convinced that I was the one who was to work with him.

When he came back the next day, for we did not share ideas at length that first night, he began at once on what he called my education. "Indoctrination" was his word. He not only wished to give me a Catholic outline of history—but he also wished to repeat over and over again his program of action; round-table discussions, houses of hospitality and agronomic universities. We were to popularize this program for immediate needs, which in itself would be the seed for a long-range program, a green revolution, by publishing a paper for the man in the street.

What Peter called round-table discussions I was already familiar enough with as meetings. I could see the necessity for them. But he wanted more than supper-table conversations; he wanted to plan meetings too for the beginnings of a school, to bring the workers and scholars together.

My whole life had been in journalism and at that time I saw the world in terms of class conflict. I did not look upon class war as something to be stirred up, I did not want to increase what was already there, but to mitigate it. When we were invited to help during a strike, we went to perform the works of mercy which include not only feeding the hungry, and visiting the imprisoned, but enlightening the ignorant and rebuking the unjust.

We started publishing *The Catholic Worker* at 436 East Fifteenth Street in May, 1933, with a first issue of 2,500 copies. By the end of the year we had a circulation of 100,000 and by 1936 it was 150,000. Parishes all over the country subscribed for the paper in bundles of 500 or more. Zealous young people took the paper out in the streets and sold it, and when they could not sell it even at one cent a copy, they gave free copies and left them in streetcar, bus, barber shop, and dentist's and doctor's offices. We got letters from all parts of the country from people who said they had picked up the paper on trains, in rooming houses. These letters thrilled and inspired the young people who came to help. We were invited to speak in schools and parishes, and often as a result of our speaking others came in to help us.

Day and night there were many meetings in the converted

barber shop which was our office. Peter had a long-term program which called for hospices, or houses of hospitality, where the works of mercy could be practiced, to combat the taking over by the state of all those services which could be built up by mutual aid; and farming communes to provide land and homes for the unemployed, whom increasing technology was piling up into the millions. In 1933, the unemployed numbered 13,000,000.

The idea of the houses of hospitality caught on quickly enough, and the cheapest, most practical way to take care of people was to rent some apartments. In New York we lived first on Fifteenth Street, then on West Charles Street, then on Mott Street for fifteen years, all together, men and women, students and workers, about twenty of us. In the summer young college girls and men came for months to help us and, in some cases, returned to their own cities to start houses of hospitality there. In this way houses started in Boston, Rochester, Milwaukee, and other cities. Within a few years there were thirty-three houses of hospitality and farms around the country.

Voluntary poverty means a good deal of discomfort in these houses of ours. Many of the houses throughout the country are without central heating and have to be warmed by stoves in winter. There are back-yard toilets for some even now. The first Philadelphia house had to use water drawn from one spigot at the end of an alley, which served half a dozen other houses. It was lit with oil lamps. It was cold and damp and so unbelievably poverty-stricken that little children coming to see who were the young people meeting there exclaimed that this could not be a Catholic place; it was too poor. We must be Communists.

How hard a thing it is to hear such criticisms made. Voluntary poverty was only found among the Communists; the Negro and white man on the masthead of our paper suggested communism; the very word "worker" made people distrust us at first.

We were not taking the position of the great mass of Catholics, who were quite content with the present in this world. They were willing to give to the poor, but they did not feel called upon to work for the things of this life for others which they themselves esteemed so lightly. Our insistence on worker-ownership, on the right of private property, on the need to deproletarize the worker, all points which had been emphasized by the Popes in their social encyclicals, made many Catholics think we were Communists in disguise, wolves in sheep's clothing.

Selling the paper in front of Macy's or St. Francis Church, or in Times Square or in front of Grand Central Station made one indeed look the fool. It was more natural to sell it along Fourteenth Street or Union Square where people were always selling or giving out literature. Once when we distributed along the water front to longshoremen, publicizing a meeting for longshoremen and seamen, one of them said, "They're always poking stuff at us, papers, posters, leaflets; first it's the Communists and then it's the Jehovah's Witnesses, and now it's the Catholics." It was a difficult job, giving out literature, or selling the paper on the streets, but when one got used to it there was joy and freedom in it too, and the comradery of those who live on the streets and talk to each other freely. We learned their point of view.

We lived with the poor, with the workers, and we knew them not just from the streets, or in mass meetings, but from years of living in the slums, in tenements, in our hospices in Washington, Baltimore, Philadelphia, Harrisburg, Pittsburgh, New York, Rochester, Boston, Worcester, Buffalo, Troy, Detroit, Cleveland, Toledo, Akron, St. Louis, Chicago, Milwaukee, Minneapolis, Seattle, San Francisco, Los Angeles, Oakland, even down into Houma, Louisiana, where Father Jerome Drolet worked with Negroes and whites, with shrimp shellers, fishermen, longshoremen and seamen.

Just as the Church has gone out through its missionaries into the most obscure towns and villages, we have gone too. Sometimes our contacts have been through the Church and sometimes through readers of our paper, through union organizers or those who needed to be organized.

We have lived with the unemployed, the sick, the unem-

ployables. The contrast between the worker who is organized
and has his union, the fellowship of his own trade to give him
strength, and those who have no organization and came in to
us on a breadline is pitiable.

My trips around the country were usually to visit our houses
of hospitality which were springing up everywhere, and also
to speak at schools. I took advantage of these trips to cover
strikes and the new organizational drive of the Congress of
Industrial Organizations.

During the course of writing about labor and capital, we
began a study club at the Mott Street headquarters. It was an
outgrowth of the seamen's strike and was started by John
Cort, a young Harvard graduate who was working with us at
the time, and Martin Wersing, a union official in the electrical
workers. Father John Monaghan and a group of other union
men joined with them in forming what they called the Association of Catholic Trade Unionists. After it had obtained its
start under our auspices, the group moved to Canal Street so
that they would have room for their meetings and could
handle the avalanche of inquiries which came to them once
they were under way.

There is so much more to the Catholic Worker movement
than labor and capital. It is people who are important, not the
masses. When I read Pope Pius XII's Christmas message, in
which he distinguished between the masses and the people, I
almost wished I had named our publication *The People,*
instead of *The Catholic Worker.*

We published many heavy articles on capital and labor, on
strikes and labor conditions, on the assembly line and all the
other evils of industrialism. But it was a whole picture we
were presenting of man and his destiny and so we emphasized
less, as the years went by, the organized labor aspect of the
paper.

Peter was not so much interested in labor as he was in work
and community. He felt that as long as men sought jobs and
wages, and accepted the assembly line and the material com-
forts the factory system brought, they would not think in
terms of community, except for that which the union brought

them. They might be gathered together in time of crisis, during strikes, but would they listen to what he said about the need for ownership and responsibility?

Every talk of Peter's about the social order led to the land. He knew the craving of the human heart for a toehold on the land, for a home of one's own, but he also knew how impossible it was to attain it except through community, through men banding together in farming communes to live to a certain extent in common, work together, own machinery together, start schools together.

Peter's plan was that groups should borrow from mutual-aid credit unions in the parish to start what he first liked to call agronomic universities, where the worker could become a scholar and the scholar a worker. Or he wanted people to give the land and money. He always spoke of giving. Those who had capital should give. Those who had labor should give that. "Love is an exchange of gifts," St. Ignatius had said.

Peter's Christian philosophy of work was this. God is our creator. God made us in His image and likeness. Therefore we are creators. He gave us a garden to till and cultivate. We become co-creators by our responsible acts, whether in bringing forth children, or producing food, furniture or clothing. The joy of creativeness should be ours. But because of the Fall the curse is laid on us of having to earn our bread by the sweat of our brows, in labor. St. Paul said that since the Fall nature itself travaileth and groaneth. So man has to contend with fallen nature in the beasts and in the earth as well as in himself. But when he overcomes the obstacles, he attains again to the joy of creativity. Work is not then all pain and drudgery.

Farms like ours began to dot the country—a dozen sprang up as Catholic Worker associates. Many others consisted of young married groups trying to restore the idea of community.

The desire was strong for private property, but even stronger for community. Man is not made to live alone. We all recognized that truth.

Peter knew that most of us not only had not been trained to disciplined work, but we did not know how to work together. We were learning through grim experience. We consoled ourselves that we might not be establishing model communities, but many a family was getting a vacation, many a sick person was nursed back to health, crowds of slum children had the run of the woods and fields for weeks, and groups of students spent happy hours discussing the green revolution.

We write a great deal about the farms in *The Catholic Worker* to share experiences with our readers and to get their advice. Realizing that we were poor like themselves, without equipment, unskilled, floundering along, we have found friends who were not afraid to tell us of their own poverty and their hard-won knowledge. We have printed letters from owners of small farms as well as from farm laborers.

I myself traveled through the Southwest from Arkansas, down through Texas and Arizona and southern California, and visited the migrant camps through the state of California. Certainly whenever we have written in *The Catholic Worker* about the conditions through the country we have tried to see and study them firsthand, and to work out a solution that would be within the means and the capacities of all.

One of the main difficulties of all these farm ventures is the lack of skills, money, and equipment; lack of leadership, too, is a factor. There could be, I believe, groups of families on the land, surrounding a chapel, disciplined by family life and daily attendance at Mass, all subject to one another, with a division of skills and labor and accepting, too, the authority of one coordinator. Ideally speaking, this should be as successful as any community of monks who maintain themselves by the labor of their hands.

However, in spite of many flaws, a community was growing up. A community of the poor, who enjoyed being together, who felt that they were embarked on a great enterprise, who had a mission. All of them understood the works of mercy. Everyone understood, in his destitution, that voluntary poverty on the part of him who possessed some of this world's goods would enable him to practice these works of mercy. All of us began to have in some slight way Peter's philosophy of poverty.

Father Pacifique Roy, a Josephite priest from Quebec who was then stationed in Baltimore, talked to us about the love of

God and what it should mean in our lives, of putting off the old man and putting on Christ. We had to aim at perfection; we had to be guided by the folly of the Cross.

His was the kind of talk to which all of us could listen, the men from the soup line, students on vacation or seminarians coming in to help for an afternoon. As Peter always dealt with the things of this world, so Father Roy always dealt with the things of the next, but the two were interwoven; time and eternity were one. We were like workers for a Utopia already living in their Utopia. We were dying and yet we lived. We were in sorrow yet rejoicing.

The last year of the war, we decided to turn one of our farms into a retreat house where people could come to study and pray, and begin to realize what it meant to be a son of God, what responsibilities such a position entailed. Our New York retreat farm was five miles west of Newburgh, New York, and it was also called Maryfarm Retreat House. Re-treatants, including family groups, came for week-ends or discussion weeks. Families vacationed in the barn, and the place was a haven of peace. Usually the "family" there was made up of more than a dozen people, with men coming off the highway for meals and a place to sleep. They, too, often stayed for a retreat or to rest on their way to look for work.

Some farming was done; vegetables were raised for the table, and there were goats, rabbits and chickens in one of the barns. We never made ends meet; there was no use keeping accounts. Now, although we no longer have Maryfarm, the same work is carried on at Peter Maurin Farm on Staten Island, New York.

It is not only for others that I must have these retreats. It is because I too am hungry and thirsty for the bread of the strong. I too must nourish myself to do the work I have under-taken; I too must drink at these good springs so that I may not be an empty cistern and unable to help others.

Peter was an apostle to this world. He loved people; he saw in them what God meant them to be, as he saw the world as God meant it to be, and loved it. He had stripped himself, but there remained work for God to do. He took from him his mind, the one thing he had left, the one thing perhaps he took delight in. He could no longer think. He could no longer make what he called his synthesis of cult, culture and cultivation.

He was sick more than five years. For the first couple of years of invalidism, he lived in Easton with us, and the last two at Maryfarm.

One thing we can be happy about, and that is that he felt he had finished his work before his mind failed. He used to say, "I have written all I have to say: I have done all I can; let the younger men take over." So he suffered but not with the feeling that there was much still that he could do.

Within the week following his funeral we had a notice served on us by a lawyer from the House of Calvary that 115 Mott Street was up for sale and that we had to find another place to live. We had lived there for fourteen years, and the house was home and the neighborhood was our village. We could not believe that we had to move, and went on in our usual routine, housekeeping, cooking, feeding, sheltering, nursing the sick and spending hours besides at correspondence. A year flew by before the blow fell. The house had been sold. We had three months to find and purchase another house. We had no money.

We all prayed, coming and going, night and day, sleeping and waking. We cannot abandon a work that is begun; we cannot walk away and leave a family which has grown up around us.

That very conviction made us look in our own neighborhood so that we would not be leaving the Bowery. Before the three months were up we found our new home on Chrystie Street, a dozen blocks away. Our new house has larger rooms than we had before. The funds came in to buy the house, supplied by our readers from all over the country in many small sums. There were two large donations of three thousand and two thousand dollars.

Our work goes on, in surroundings more spacious and comfortable than those on Mott Street, but our poverty is more acute if it is less obvious. We have not yet caught up with the bills of last year. As I write this there is less than a hundred dollars in the bank, the line of men stretches to the corner, and our households here and at Peter Maurin Farm comprise seventy-five people or more. How can we go on? We are as sure as we ever were that God can multiply the loaves, as He has sheltered the homeless these many years.

Truth Makes Us Free

JAMES M. O'NEILL [1]

THE writing and lecturing which I have done in recent years on subjects of special interest to American Catholics have grown out of my experience in education. So far as I can trace the influences which have been most important in my professional life, I think that any contribution I have made to a better understanding of the Catholic Church, or to a defense of her doctrine and her history, is due in large part to my long activity as a teacher and coach in argumentation and debate. Following this training and life-long experience in controversy, and a great respect for competent controversy on either side of any question, came my experience in the American Civil Liberties Union, and arising directly and traceably

[1] James M. O'Neill has had a long and distinguished career as teacher, author and lecturer. He has taught on every level from the primary grade in a rural school to the graduate seminar in large universities. He has been head of the Department of Speech at the University of Wisconsin, the University of Michigan, and Brooklyn College. One of the founders and the first president of the National Speech Association, he also founded and served for six years as editor of the *Quarterly Journal of Speech* and has contributed articles to many secular and Catholic periodicals. Throughout his career spanning forty-six years in secular education, Dr. O'Neill has been a loyal son and a worthy representative of the Church. But in recent years he has made an outstanding contribution to the Catholic cause in America by writing *Catholicism and American Freedom*, which is a direct and eminently successful refutation of the specious charges contained in Paul Blanshard's *American Freedom and Catholic Power*. Dr. O'Neill's other well-known books are *Religion and Education under the Constitution, Catholics in Controversy* and *The Catholic in Secular Education*. Now retired from teaching, he resides at Lakeville, Connecticut, and devotes his time to writing and lecturing.

136

out of that experience came the writing and lecturing which
have engaged most of my time in recent years.

My pre-college schooling was in public schools. Then I
spent four years in Dartmouth College, and after graduating
in 1907, had a year of further study in Harvard Law School
and two summer sessions in the University of Chicago Law
School. My forty-six years in teaching, from which I retired in
1952, were made up of forty years in public education and six
years in non-Catholic, private education.

I was born on a fifty-acre farm in Victor, New York, which
was left, with a mortgage, to my mother who became a widow
with six children at thirty-five. Still, the six of us had an
unusually happy childhood and lived to achieve a happy and
successful maturity. There was no Catholic school in Victor
or in any of the neighboring villages, but we did have Catholic
teachers. On entering high school I was particularly impressed
by the young, enthusiastic, superlatively intelligent principal,
George Ray Wicker, a graduate of Geneseo Normal School
and Cornell University. This contact grew into one of the
most influential factors in my life, and perhaps set the course
of my vocation as early as 1897, when he chose me to represent
the high school in a local contest in public speaking, selected
my declamation, and coached me in its delivery. I won first
prize.

Then our family moved to Canandaigua, New York. After
graduation came my first teaching experience in a tiny settle-
ment near the head of Canandaigua Lake. It was a typical
country school, all the grades together from primary to high
school with a single teacher. Though it was a happy year, I
exchanged my career for various jobs, and then settled more
permanently to one as freight clerk with the Northern Central
Railroad. There it was part of my job to collect the mail on
Sunday and take it to the office. This trivial errand is
mentioned because of a late train one Sunday morning, an
incident from which seemed to spring many important events
of my mature life.

As I watched the people getting off, I recognized one of
them as Mr. Wicker. It was a joyful reunion. Before long I

was telling him of my hopes and plans for more education when I had enough money. His response was completely characteristic, encouraging, hopeful, practical. He pointed out to me that a great deal of money would not be required, and a year later I was registered at Dartmouth College, beginning the first of four of the most pleasant years of my life. Added to the joy of learning, there was the pleasure of new friends and professors, the expert guidance and encouragement of my old teacher and friend.

All too quickly it was spring, 1907, a few weeks from graduation. I lacked only two credits for the A.B. degree when the principal of the Lyndon Institute at Lyndonville, Vermont, came to Dartmouth in search of a senior who could drop out of college for six weeks to teach in the Institute. The Dean recommended me. I took the job after being assured by Professor Emery, the head of the English Department, that I could pass his course in Shakespeare without attending classes for the rest of the term.

This teaching assignment was followed by an appointment as an English master in the Hotchkiss School in Lakeville, Connecticut, which lasted for two years, and which might have continued indefinitely, except that my own college invited me to return to teach, largely in argumentation and debate, and I could not resist. However, after a year of teaching at Dartmouth I again became a full-time student at Harvard Law School, with summer sessions at Chicago Law School. I particularly wanted certain courses in order to be better prepared for the teaching of argumentation.

Again my plans were dramatically changed. In 1913 I was offered the headship of the Department of Public Speaking at the University of Wisconsin with the rank of associate professor. Though I gave up all thought of going further in law when I accepted the position, the knowledge of legal principles and procedures which I had learned were of inestimable value.

I spent fourteen years as head of the Department of Public Speaking at Wisconsin, which by that time had been changed to the Department of Speech. I was married in Madison, and my six children were born there.

In the fall of 1927 I went to a similar position at the University of Michigan, Ann Arbor, where I stayed until 1935. Michigan was close to the bottom of the great financial depression of that period, and there came a time when the state of Michigan could not pay its bills, including the salaries at the University, and scrip was issued to state employees to buy food and certain other necessities. For a large family like ours this became increasingly difficult, and when, in the spring of 1935, I was offered the headship of the Department of Speech at Brooklyn College, one of the municipal colleges of the city of New York, I was glad to accept.

In my years of college and university teaching I knew a number of Catholic faculty members, and I lived in an atmosphere that I believe was as free from any anti-Catholic prejudice as you could find in America. I realized in those years that there are non-Catholic administrators in high positions, particularly in public education, who welcome an opportunity to bring to their faculties competent Catholic scholars and teachers. I believe that there are probably scores of such administrators throughout the United States, and that the number of Catholics on the faculties of secular colleges could be tremendously increased if young Catholics of intellectual ability and good personality would prepare themselves for and seek positions in public higher education. There is probably no position in America where a Catholic can exercise more beneficent influence, not by picking quarrels or making himself offensive as a propagandist, but simply by being there and occasionally answering a sincere question from someone who would like to know something about the Church and its doctrines.

Most of my writing and lecturing in recent years has been argumentative, controversial. I know that some people, in reviewing books or commenting on public lectures, use the word *argumentative* as a derogatory adjective. Argumentation is simply one of the great divisions of rhetoric and, incidentally, the one of the four divisions which covers a great deal of the other three—description, narration, and exposition. Most great speeches, most great editorials have been argumen-

tative. Controversy (argumentation and debate) is the life
blood of any free society; it is the manner in which a free
society, as a society, lives and grows and transacts its affairs.
It is a matter of great satisfaction to me that my speaking and
writing are largely argumentative.

Because I like this activity and prepared myself to teach it,
it is easy to see why I went into the field of controversy; however, there are one or two specific incidents which led me
directly into it. Shortly after I came to Brooklyn College, I
joined the American Civil Liberties Union to take a place on
its National Committee on Academic Freedom. I served on
that Committee for twelve years, the last four as chairman. In
my work on that Committee I became aware of the tremendous lack of information among all sorts of Americans,
and of the many false assumptions accepted as truths in regard
to civil liberties and the Bill of Rights. There developed some
friendly differences of opinion in the Committee concerning
the history and meaning of the First Amendment.

One of the members of the Committee was Dr. Vivian
Thayer, Director of the Ethical Culture Schools in New York
City. I had known Dr. Thayer ever since we had been colleagues at the University of Wisconsin. He is one of the outstanding spokesmen for militant secularism in the United
States, and he took the position that the First Amendment was
designed to, and did, provide for absolute, complete, separation of Church and State, meaning no cooperative contact of
any kind between a government agency and religion. I dif-
fered with him, and thought him totally mistaken.

He was much interested in arranging a program for the 75th
anniversary of the founding of the Ethical Culture Schools;
and since he was in favor of free speech and was glad to have
the opposition state its case, he graciously asked me to speak
on that occasion on the meaning of the First Amendment.
My talk was well received, and I later developed my remarks
into an article which was published by the distinguished
Jewish monthly, *Commentary,* in June of 1947, under the
title "Church, Schools, and the Constitution." This article
attracted considerable attention, and I decided to write a book

along the same lines, as this would give me an opportunity to present the well-documented evidence upon which my position was based, far too ample to be included in a brief magazine article. The result was the volume *Religion and Education under the Constitution,* published by Harper and Brothers in 1949.

I had been gathering notes and material for some time with the possibility in mind of writing a book in regard to the relation of American Catholics to the Bill of Rights, or to civil liberties. This project was still in a nebulous state when *The Nation* announced Mr. Blanshard's articles on the Catholic Chuch. I sent in a short-term subscription to *The Nation* in order to get these articles. They were absurd. In fact, after reading the first two or three I skipped the rest; I felt sorry for anyone who could write such stuff and for a magazine that could publish it. I decided that few, if any, literate persons would pay any attention to such writing.

Then the book appeared, Paul Blanshard's *American Freedom and Catholic Power,* published by the Beacon Press in Boston. Immediately reviews began to appear praising this book as scholarly, and marvelously well-documented. One commentator said that every statement in it had been checked and double-checked by distinguished Catholic scholars. In other words, from the reviews and comments, it seemed to me that it must be quite different from his articles in *The Nation*. I bought the book and read it all. It was, if anything, worse than the articles; perhaps mainly because there was more of it.

The Blanshard articles had most of the worst faults of argument known to students of rhetoric from Aristotle down to the latest high school text. Particularly evident were the inaccurate use of words, unsupported assertions, inaccurate interpretations, the apparent absence of information, the offering of inept remarks of individual Catholics as OFFICIAL CATHOLIC DOCTRINE, and the repetition of charges which have been answered again and again. All these faults were in the book in profusion.

I felt I must answer it, and I knew I could. I have been a practicing Catholic all my life. I have been interested in

Catholic affairs, a reader of Catholic periodicals, a listener to Catholic sermons, and I knew Mr. Blanshard's thesis was false. His discussion of the belief and practice of American Catholics, which he presented in support of his thesis, was so biased and inaccurate as to be substantially worthless. Anyone, of any religion, or none, with some knowledge of the Church's doctrines knew Mr. Blanshard's thesis was false; and anyone with elementary knowledge of the principles of argument and proof should have known that Mr. Blanshard did not prove his case.

If the book was so bad, why take it so seriously? The answer is that it was praised and promoted by men who, on account of the positions they occupied, and the ideals they advocated, should have been expected to expose its anti-religious, anti-Catholic bias, its basic freedom-smothering philosophy, and its erroneous scholarship. The betrayal of American scholarship by the encomiums heaped on Mr. Blanshard's book has done more to produce what have been called the "tensions" between Catholic and non-Catholic Americans than all of Mr. Blanshard's inaccuracies and insults put together.

I was not asked or commissioned to undertake the task of replying to Mr. Blanshard's book by anyone representing the Catholic Church or any Catholic agency, organization or institution. I wrote, not as a philosopher or theologian, but as a Catholic layman who enjoyed answering such vicious slander against the Church.

My purpose was not to convert my readers to Catholicism—my objective not that all should believe in the Catholic Church, but that no one should believe in Mr. Blanshard. And I wanted to make it easier for Americans to live in harmony and freedom by exposing for them the sham scholarship, the distorted, false Blanshard thesis by accurately placing beside it the truth about the doctrines of the Church. I was delighted when my answer was published in the volume *Catholicism and American Freedom* by Harper and Brothers in 1952.

I am again delighted to contribute this chapter to another book recording the apostolic lives of my fellow Catholics, and I would impress upon my readers the words of the great

Pontiff, Leo XIII, spoken on the opening of the Vatican archives to the scholars of the world:

"The first law of history is, not to dare to utter falsehood; the second, not to fear to speak the truth."

Take to the Air

A. DOROTHY ARTHUR [1]

THE voice on the telephone said urgently, "Could you help us with Sunday's television show? We need a crozier-holder desperately."

Bewildered, the high school sophomore echoed, "A crozier-holder?"

"That's right. We're presenting Bishop-elect Edward J. Schlotterback, O.S.F.S., and a demonstration on the rite of consecration with a whole bunch of Oblates of St. Francis de Sales, and we have to have someone to hold on to the crozier."

"Oh! A *crozier*," she said, light dawning.

"It's a present," the voice went on. "Worth a lot of money. We can't just stand it in a corner."

"O.K.," she said. "I'll be at the studio Sunday."

And she was. All through the Catholic Television Guild program on "Bishop to the Hottentots," a presentation on

---

[1] A. Dorothy Arthur of Wilmington, Delaware, was one of the four original members of the Catholic Forum of the Air and has been active in that group since 1939. When the Catholic Television Guild of Wilmington was organized in 1952, she was elected its first chairman and is at present a member of the Board of Directors. At the charter convention of the Catholic Broadcasters Association at Boston in 1948, she was named coordinator of the C.B.A., a post which she held for seven years and for which she became ineligible in 1955 only by her election to the Board of Directors. In addition to being a member of the Board she has served as secretary-treasurer of the C.B.A. for the past two years. Miss Arthur insists that her activities in radio and television have been only a small part in a cooperative effort and that she is here but reporting for the groups of which she is a member.

144

what it means to be a missionary bishop expressed in the person of a well-known Wilmington, Delaware, resident, the girl's sole task was to hold the crozier, hand it to the Oblate enacting the duties of master of ceremonies, and then take it back from him when the scene was over.

She was essential to the program.

If Catholic Action can be understood to be the participation of the laity in the work of the hierarchy, then radio and television offer a comparatively new and fascinating facet of the lay apostolate.

If St. Paul were alive today, he'd probably be preaching over the biggest network possible. If so, he'd have to be backed up with a staff. Throughout the country radio and television programs under Catholic auspices are attempting to reach people who would never open a door to a priest, possibly not even to St. Paul. Every program must be approved, at least implicitly, by St. Paul's modern counterpart, the bishop in whose jurisdiction it originates. For many of the live programs, and some of the filmed and transcribed ones as well, the lay people are the "staff."

Now the fact is that the "crozier-holder" above had appeared a few months earlier as the lead in an original television drama, *The Cheat,* a comedy exploring the morality of cheating in school, on the income tax, on the family budget, and in other sensitive areas. She carried off the part on a maximum power TV station in an audience area of five and a half million people.

A press analyst for a large corporation wrote the script. The mother of two small children directed it. A junior executive played the father. A paint salesman helped put up the set. A UNIVAC operator moved furniture. The mother of a member of the cast, watching the program, commented that the lamp shade in the set looked exactly like the one out on her porch. It should. It was.

This appeared as another of the telecasts presented by the Catholic Television Guild, which for the past year has been producing weekly half-hour programs. Before that it was every other week. Like quite a few other Catholic radio and television efforts around the country, three elements make this lay production possible: the approval of the local Ordinary, the availability of sustaining time on the local station, and the continuous diligence of a reliable group.

Even where there is a diocesan director of radio and television—a comparatively new post—the demands of multi-radio program production, to say nothing of television, make a one-man staff out of the question. Often the priest assigned to this responsibility accepts it as one more task in a schedule that is already heavy on time-and-a-half assignments. Besides, the studios are more comfortable when they know a "group" is there to back up commitments in the event of one person's necessary absence. That's where the lay people come in. . . . Indeed, in more cases than a few, it is the lay group which takes the initiative and then persuades a priest to supervise its efforts. Professionals in the industry repeatedly make themselves available to advise priests and groups on intelligent methods of setting up shows. Volunteers help in everything from script writing to running the mimeograph machine or providing music, or producing the art work, or prompting the actors, or just the no-glamor and no-recognition job of holding the crozier.

These Catholic radio and television programs come in all sizes and shapes. At the 1956 meeting of the Catholic Broadcasters Association in Boston, the service organization through which a good percentage of them exchange scripts, ideas and encouragement, national and local programs of dozens of formats were represented.

They were warned: "Beware of the person sitting on your right. You have fallen in among thieves. You have come here full of zeal for your own presentation—the broadcast of the Mass for shut-ins, or the daily recitation of the Rosary, or a discussion series on what Catholics believe, or book chats on television, or interviews with interesting persons who demonstrate that Catholics are good people in the community, or straight dramas—and you know what? That apparently honest individual alongside you is quite likely to pick your mind, milk you for every detail and steal your idea for use in his own diocese.

"And even worse is the person on your left. This is the one who is so convinced that his program is the most effective that he is likely to thrust it upon you whether you want it or not."

Such enthusiasm is typical. But the refrain at the C.B.A. meeting was: "Why aren't there more Catholic programs on the air? If we can do these programs, so can others."

In smaller communities, or on newly-opened stations in particular, time is not impossible to obtain. It becomes markedly easier to get if the "package" offered the studio is of good quality, reliable regularity, wrapped in consistent promotion and followed up with letters of appreciation to the studio. Name any one of these jobs a lay person cannot do!

Chats with others in C.B.A. prove that there are dozens of ways lay people started (or were trapped into) working with a Catholic radio or television production. This is how it happened in Wilmington, Delaware.

At a public meeting at the Ursuline Academy back in 1939, a local station manager offered time for a Catholic program. Promptly, an Ursuline Mother accepted. Just as promptly, she tagged a busy young attorney and assured him he certainly would like to assume responsibility for it. He gulped, fumbled his opportunity to refuse, and that was the beginning of weekly programs by the Catholic Forum of the Air. As of this writing it's in its eighteenth year.

The attorney recruited "volunteers" weekly until he determined that a permanent group was the only hope of maintaining sanity as well as the program. He persuaded an insurance broker, a salesman, and a girl still in college. From these four, it expanded to include school teachers, secretaries, chemists, married and single, young and older. Since none had experience in writing or speaking for radio they did a lot of studying and learning together. They plagiarized from only the most reliable sources. When their 400th consecutive weekly program came in sight, one of the girls looked up to observe that that was a lot.

"Why not tell someone else about us?"

So the Forum posed for a picture—the girl was a public relations writer—and released a story. The next thing you know—fan mail!

Well, not exactly. The story appeared in the *Denver Register* and elsewhere. A dozen, then twenty, then a hundred or so people wrote to this little lay group.

They didn't say, "Wonderful! Good for you!" No. None, except, in a manner of speaking, the Holy Father. The Forum wasn't sure how it happened, but the mail brought a letter from the Apostolic Delegate telling them the Holy Father had granted an Apostolic Benediction to the Forum on its 400th program.

But the rest of the people . . . they wrote:

"Please send us enough dramatic scripts to start a program." (The Forum had never done drama by then, only discussions and documentaries.)

"I'm a missionary priest and I've exhausted my present ideas in the past two years of writing my own talks. Please send me a series of 15-minute talks." (But the Forum was a lay group, and didn't do straight talks.)

"I'd like to accept the local station's offer of a fifteen-minute morning devotion spot. Please send me scripts suitable for a largely non-Catholic audience." (Oh, dear, the Forum had nothing like this on file either.)

We protested to one another that we weren't the ones to ask. But who was?

Out of our dismay at seeing all this need, an idea dawned. The girl who got us into all this observed: "That priest who's done two years—why don't we suggest he send his scripts to the one who wants to get started? In that way at least one gets what he needs, and the other gets the satisfaction of giving."

But this meant writing dozens of letters.

Again, our public relations member dreamed up an "easy" solution.

"Let's put out a Newsletter," she suggested. "We'll abstract letters people write us giving the offers and the wants and list complete names and addresses, We can mail these, mimeo-

graphed, for one cent. Then we can tell all these inquirers,
'Don't ask us! Ask one another.'"

This was the birth of the Catholic Forum of the Air *Newsletter,* top circulation 167.

Forum members came early for rehearsals for Sunday's program and engaged in busy little sessions of envelope stuffing
and stamp licking. Postage money was raised through bake-
sales.

Eventually, some correspondents did inquire, "How do you
go about starting a lay, local program like yours?"

At last! The only question the Forum could answer from
experience. We printed a leaflet called, "Take to the Air," and
have since given away about a thousand copies. In that first
year we saw three other groups, one in Pennsylvania, one in
Vermont and one in Wisconsin, start their own "Forums." It
was wonderful. All of a sudden the letter writing and envelope
stuffing seemed like no work at all.

But this was just a whisper on the air waves. In July, 1947,
the Catholic Forum of the Air *Newsletter* innocently inquired:
"What are you doing in August? Be on hand for the start of a
National Association of Catholic Broadcasters. The time:
August 16 and 17; the place: Fordham University.

". . . Many of you whom we've contacted have expressed
interest in it too. The advantages of such an organization
would be great. . . . We will have a good opportunity to
start . . . this summer. . . . This is what you are invited to
attend."

Fordham had given us a roof. Friends passed the word.
Some important Catholic broadcasters not on the *Newsletter*
mailing list were especially invited. On a day forever to be
remembered for its heat and humidity, more than a hundred
people sat down together to explore exchanging scripts, music,
ideas, experiences—all in the cause of increasing and improv-
ing Catholic communication.

If the members of the Forum, surely among the youngest
there, had paused to look around, they might have been
amazed at the geographic distribution, the variety and the experience represented in that room. These Catholic broadcasters

had come together and were actually meeting one another for the first time. The occasion had been contrived by an entirely average assortment of lay men and women who had intended only to try to find the "easy" way to do things.

But none of them had time to contemplate the alert attention in this quite distinguished assemblage. We were all too busy mimeographing the agenda just fast enough to keep ahead of the clock . . . and in finding faces that went with the signatures on the letters we'd been receiving.

Suddenly, one voice asserted: "This is impossible! Handling a script exchange, correspondence, and issuing a Newsletter can't be done without a paid staff and proper office arrangements. There is no money for this. Therefore, it can't be done."

The Forum members blinked. Looked at one another. One arose and replied, "But it has been done."

It had. The Forum had done it during the past year.

So the broadcasters at the Fordham meeting appointed a temporary committee to hold together a temporary Catholic Broadcasters Association. The Catholic Forum of the Air *Newsletter* became the temporary C.B.A. *Newsletter* until the Charter Convention of C.B.A. in Boston in 1948. There, as guests of His Excellency, the Most Reverend Richard J. Cushing, Archbishop of Boston, the Catholic broadcasters adopted a constitution and elected a Board of Directors. C.B.A. has been growing ever since, with laymen forming an appropriate part of an association whose board has been populated by diocesan clergy, members of religious societies and communities, nuns, and a brother in religion in addition to the laity.

The Wilmington Forum members settled back to turning out weekly programs, mimeographing a fair number of their scripts and offering them through C.B.A. as available to others on request, in the same way as many other groups throughout the country used C.B.A.'s clearinghouse services.

But not too long afterwards, His Excellency, the Most Reverend Edmond J. FitzMaurice, our own beloved Bishop of Wilmington, came out of a luncheon where several forms of Catholic Action had been discussed. He tapped one of the

Forum members on the shoulder, held up an admonishing finger: "Television! Don't forget television."

She cringed slightly. Months earlier, the brand new local TV station had offered time to the Forum. It had space for local originations. But who knew anything about television? And wasn't radio enough work now?

But when the Bishop gives the word. . . .

In 1950, the Catholic Television Guild collected itself. One of the Forum members, a personnel supervisor for a chemical concern professionally, took leave of absence from the radio apostolate to push ahead in "spare time" television. She subsequently escaped from this work by joining the Order of St. Ursula. When she left, seven people—four men and three women—were elected to a Board under the new constitution for the Television Guild to try to handle the job she had been doing.

Both the Forum and the Guild are under the supervision of their respective chaplain-censors appointed by the Bishop. Both try to keep replenishing their memberships by recruiting likely people whose zeal or talent makes them good prospects. Both give much credit to St. Gabriel for the fact that despite the usual reasons for dropping out of such apostolic endeavors, enough personnel is on hand to keep the scripts coming.

The chaplain for the radio group was once one of its members. In addition, the priest who is now director of the Society for the Propagation of the Faith in Wilmington was one of the original four in the Forum, the insurance broker. Another Forum alumnus is the present director of the Confraternity of Christian Doctrine in our diocese. All three of these priests appear with the television Guild nowadays. In fact, the Guild has persuaded a fair percentage of the Wilmington clergy that they and what they have to say will go very well on TV.

Indeed, there was a time when the biggest problem the radio group had was that key people kept "deserting" to the religious life, as we said when we accused them of going just to get out of writing the two scripts they had promised for the next series. But remember the young lawyer who was tagged to "take responsibility" for the original radio series back in 1939? His daughter, a high school senior now, has just co-authored and produced her first half-hour drama for the Catholic Forum of the Air. Now that the second generation is starting there is some hope that the Wilmington effort in the apostolate of the airwaves is finally getting on firm footing.

What has been and is being done in Wilmington can be duplicated by lay groups across the country. In fact, many similar groups have already started, and a new day is dawning for Catholic radio and television. Technical knowledge can be acquired as time goes on; experience is the best teacher, and professional people are usually eager to act as advisors. What is needed is enthusiasm, which is another word for zeal, perseverance—and vision.

Radio and television present an unparalleled opportunity and a challenge. With the command of Christ to preach His Gospel to every creature ringing in their ears, more and more Catholic broadcasters are accepting the challenge and seizing the opportunity. Non-Catholics, and particularly the unchurched millions, will rarely enter a Catholic church or read a Catholic periodical. But in the privacy of their homes they will and do tune in programs presenting Catholic truth attractively and entertainingly on radio and television. Some such programs are already available on the national, regional, and local levels, but many more are needed. These will be provided only when more Catholics take to the air.

Lay Missionary

VIOLET NEVILE [1]

To LOOK back over one's life trying to pick out those events or circumstances which had some bearing on later developments is an entertaining pastime—but it seems to me it is not always a very rewarding one. It is true that I can see factors in my childhood and adolescence which have probably contributed to my vocation in an international society of lay missionaries but, at the same time, I see such different circumstances in the lives of others who have arrived at the same vocation that I can only conclude that God leads us all by His own secret ways which defy analysis. Perhaps the greatest contributing influence in anyone's choice of vocation is his family background. But, exception made of all that was immediately connected with my family, I believe I can see two factors which probably influenced me the most. The first was in childhood, the second when I was already grown up.

The first was a man who was private tutor to my sisters and me over the period of a year or more, when we were all between the ages of twelve and sixteen. He lived with his wife in a cottage near our home, and when he was not trying to

[1] Violet Nevile is a member of a lay missionary society, the International Catholic Auxiliaries, and the experiences of her own life suggest just how international she is. Born in France and reared in England, she lived for a time in South Africa, trained as a lay missionary in Belgium, then acted for several years as director of the Training Center of the International Catholic Auxiliaries at 1103 North Dearborn Street, Chicago 10, Illinois. She is now vice-president of the Auxiliaries and works from the headquarters of the organization in Brussels.

get some learning into our inattentive heads he was performing good works in the village in which we lived. True, many other people I knew, including my own family, performed good works, but this man had a zest about him which was different. He had been a Protestant clergyman, and after his conversion he and his wife had worked in a mission in Southern Rhodesia, Africa. Their missionary zeal was still with them, and they gave me my first experience with lay people bent on retrieving lapsed Catholics and of converting people to the Faith. In other words, they were the first "lay apostles" I ever met who impressed me as such. Much later on, when I was casting about for some way to work in the missions as a lay person, it was the fact that they had done so that assured me that it was possible. And I needed that assurance, for the reception met by my first tentative inquiries was far from encouraging. The influence of this man, however, was by no means sufficient to give me a personal desire for the lay apostolate. It took much more than that.

At the age of twenty-three, after World War II, I was in Johannesburg, South Africa, living with my brother and trying, quite deliberately, to have a good time. I was not succeeding, and I became more and more impressed with the emptiness and the discontent in the lives of the people around me as well as in my own. For the discontent in my own life I had no excuse and I knew it—but for them it was different. For the first time in my life I had a close experience of paganism—and it sickened me. It also shocked me into a sense of responsibility. Apart from my brother I was the only Catholic that most of these people knew . . . and what kind of witness to Christ was I being for them? Almost at the same time I realized the inadequacy of my response to the gift of Faith, the desperate need for dedicated Christians who would stay in the world, and a personal call from God to give myself to Him. I need hardly say that all this did not strike me overnight, nor was I able to accept the implications for myself without a struggle. But by the time I left Johannesburg I had made up my mind to serve the Church as a missionary and, if it were physically possible, as a lay missionary.

It was on the way back to England from South Africa that I questioned missionaries with long beards about the possibilities of lay workers cooperating with them, and was laughed at for my pains. At that time I felt vaguely, but strongly, the need of belonging to a group, but I remember making up my mind nevertheless that if there were no group in existence I would get a job that would take me back to Africa. There, I was sure, I would find someone willing to make use of me. Later, I do not know why, my thinking changed, and I told the Sacred Heart nun to whom I went for advice that I wanted to be a missionary and if there were no other way, "I would even become a religious!" Fortunately for my particular vocation she knew that there was another way, and she showed it to me when she gave me a mission magazine in which was a five-line advertisement about the International Catholic Auxiliaries. That was the end of my searching and the beginning of a very different life. In point of fact, although it had seemed long from the day in Johannesburg when I accepted the Lord's invitation to follow Him, to the day I found the Auxiliaries, it was something less than a year.

It was another year before I found myself in Brussels, Belgium, to begin my training as a missionary. And what a world was opened before my eyes! The first thing I discovered was the Mystical Body! Why had no one ever told me of this before, I wondered. But looking back, I realized I probably had been told but just had never been aware of it in all its beauty. This was a discovery which was very practical as well as theoretical, for there were Auxiliaries from fifteen different countries in the house, all training to work as missionaries in this one international society. The theory underlying "diversity in unity," fraternal love and cooperation, and the universality of the Church took on flesh and was brought home to us by the simple fact of living together. Our countries—France and Viet Nam, for instance, or England and Germany—often had histories of bitter conflicts, yet we were all united in one campaign for one kingdom—the kingdom of Christ.

I learned to love the missions, too. Although I had determined to give my life to them, actually I knew next to nothing about the work. But here I learned that the missions represent a vital part of the growth of the Mystical Body, not just a remote apostolate in foreign lands. I also learned that the average "mission country" is far removed from the savage jungle of popular imagination and that many Asians and Africans have a refinement and culture which put Westerners to shame. I had often met "Orientalists" who collected beautiful Chinese jades and porcelains, but I had never met any one of them who really loved the people who made these works of art and longed with all his heart to bring the Chinese to Christ and Christ to the Chinese. In South Africa I had met many native Africans, most of them simple, uneducated people, a few cultured and ambitious. Nowhere in Africa had I met more than a handful of white people who really liked and respected Africans as equals. Here, among the Auxiliaries, I met such an atmosphere of respect and love for all men combined with a realistic appreciation of the differences and difficulties between us, that it struck me that this was the authentic Christian spirit. This was what I had been looking for.

By the time I joined the Auxiliaries, in 1950, the Society had been in existence a little over twelve years. The two teams of workers who had gone to China after World War II had just returned to Belgium. They had been forced out of China again by the murder of one of their number in Nanking in March, 1949, and by the rapid progress of the Communists. There were already two teams doing social and medical work in the Belgian Congo, Africa, and another was working with Arab refugees in Palestine. (At the moment of writing, 1956, there are altogether fourteen teams of Auxiliaries working in social, medical and educational work in Asia and Africa.) When I arrived in Brussels in May, 1950, Yvonne Poncelet, the foundress and president, was in the Holy Land. On her return she announced that the Auxiliaries there would stop their work, as the first emergency was over, and would give themselves entirely to a study of the language and the customs of the country before embarking on any other activities. Their basic training in Arabic was going to last two years! This was

another shock, for it had never really occurred to me before
how much study a language could demand. Nor had I realized
how important it was for us as lay missionaries to be
thoroughly well equipped in the natural and technical aspects
of our work. It was a lesson to me that we should spare no
pains to lay good foundations for our work. Goodwill alone
is not enough.

But I learned something else as well from Yvonne's account
of the Auxiliaries' work in the Near East. This was the lesson
of adaptation. For the Auxiliaries had become Greek Catholics
in accord with the predominance of the Greek rite in that
area. It is one thing to work and communicate with people
in a new language; it is quite another to pray in it, adopting
different rituals and gestures. Of course, the underlying realities of the Mass and sacraments are the same, but what we see
and hear and feel is the expression of a different mentality,
and it takes a long time for it to become ours. Adaptation to
a different nationality is not easy, and the full implications of
it were brought home to me by this wonderful example. In
this the Auxiliaries follow Father Vincent Lebbe, the famous
missionary instrumental in their founding, who said, "If Paul
had remained a Jew who would have led us out of darkness?
If I wanted to remain a European I should be a corpse. One
only knows men by becoming one of them, one can only win
them by giving oneself."

Toward the end of 1950 and the beginning of 1951 Yvonne
Poncelet and several other Auxiliaries came to Canada and
the United States. Their first purpose was to continue the
training of those of us new to the Society and, later, to establish a second Training Center. I was among those sent to
continue their training, and eventually, in 1953, I was assigned
to begin a new Training Center in Chicago.

My first task was to make the Auxiliaries known, so that
when we opened our training program there would be some
girls asking to be trained. The biggest problem facing us in
this was simply the size of the United States and the shortage
of means. We could not hope to be known by everyone, and
so we had to make a choice. Basing my itinerary on a few

invitations to speak before groups about our work and on three mammoth mission exhibits sponsored by the Society for the Propagation of the Faith, I spent the next few months travelling around the country in a secondhand Dodge, handing out literature and answering questions about lay missionaries.

This was the best preparation for running a Training Center that I could have had for, as I soon discovered, it was not enough to have a few pat answers ready about the needs of the Church and the way we hoped to respond to those needs. Some people took a lot of convincing, and I could never convince them with ready-made replies. Also, their questions found the weak spots in my own knowledge and thinking, so that I was forced to think and pray about my vocation more than I ever had before. In this way I came to understand it more deeply and to be more than ever convinced of its value and need for myself and for the Church. When we finally opened our training program in October, 1953, I had already experienced the tremendous open-heartedness of American Catholics. I had been helped at every turn and felt I had friends in all the cities I had visited. We had six candidates for our first year of training, and gradually America is taking its place as one of the countries with a large representation in the Auxiliaries.

Since 1950, I have had plenty of opportunity to read and think and learn more about the whole field of the lay apostolate. There are many forms of it today, and each variety seems to have been prepared by the Holy Ghost for its own particular work. But they also have very much in common. Rather than give a broad general description, therefore, of the actual work we do, I prefer to mention a couple of points which might help to make clear the particular contribution which our Society has to give to the whole field.

First, I think it offers to the missionary Church an instrument specially adapted to the various needs to be filled in a growing Christian community. It gives, at the same time, the *flexibility* necessary for these changing needs and the *stability* needed for a fruitful apostolate. The rules of the Society are few and are planned with these two characteristics in mind. The "work-unit" is a team composed of from three to six girls placed under obedience to their mission bishop for all that concerns their apostolate in his diocese. This guarantees that the one who knows best what is needed, the bishop in his own diocese, is the one who makes the final decisions about the work. The only task of the Society is to ensure that the Auxiliaries really are everything that the statutes require them to be. For this reason it has undertaken to train them in various professional fields, recognizing the need for skilled technicians, as well as giving spiritual training and continued support and encouragement for the spiritual life of each member.

Second, it seems to me that the Auxiliaries have a substantial contribution to make in that they offer a vocation, a fully dedicated life, to the increasing number of young women who are drawn to the full apostolate but not to the religious life. The spiritual demands of this type of dedication are just as great as for religious life, the gift of oneself to Almighty God is just as complete. The obedience, love, humility and courage required are, if possible, even more necessary in a life with the minimum of formal regulations and restrictions such as ours. A failure to reach the standards set is just as tragic and even more noticeable because of the smallness of the teams and their close association with their fellow-men.

It is becoming more and more obvious that this type of dedication has an important role to play in the Church. There are many indications of it, the most significant being the unprecedented encouragement of the Holy Father and other members of the hierarchy. Those who live the evangelical counsels as lay people certainly have no monopoly on sanctity nor are they the only ones doing something constructive for the Church. But one thing they, and only they, can do is to express to the world at large the primacy of the spiritual realities we all live by and the possibility of living them fully as laymen. And how sorely needed this testimony is!

If there was one thing I learned in South Africa it was that the example of Christian living coming to the average layman from one of his own kind has a powerful impact. That is how the Lord showed me His need. That is why I chose to remain a lay person.

In God's Service

DALE FRANCIS [1]

I WANT to tell this as simply as I can.

I am a convert to the Catholic Church. Long before I even knew of the Church I wanted to serve God. Because of this desire I became a Protestant minister and served a small Ohio congregation for several years. And yet I was dissatisfied, for there was something I sought that I did not have as a Protestant. In 1945, I became a Catholic. I knew then—and I've never had a split second's doubt since—that the Catholic Church was the Church established by Christ, and I knew that I wanted to use what talents God had given me to serve Him and His Church.

I was in the army when I became a Catholic. When I got my discharge early in 1946, I returned to journalism, for before

[1] Dale Francis, though still a young man, has had a varied and interesting career. Born in 1917, he became a newspaper reporter at the age of fifteen, a Methodist minister at twenty-one. Converted to Catholicism while serving in the U.S. Army, he entered on a new career of service to God and the Church. Shortly after his discharge in 1946, he went to the diocese of Raleigh, North Carolina, to found a Catholic weekly newspaper and to become executive secretary of the North Carolina Catholic Laymen's Association. Later he moved to the University of Notre Dame, where he was appointed Director of Publications and where he established the University of Notre Dame Press. Returning to North Carolina in 1951, Mr. Francis opened a Catholic information center, the Sign of the Cross, in the city of Charlotte. For more than five years he has written a weekly column for *Our Sunday Visitor*. In all these projects Mr. Francis has had the encouragement, support, and collaboration of his wife, the former Barbara Hoole. They now live in San Miguel de los Banos, Matanzas, Cuba, where they are continuing their apostolic work.

I had been a minister and after, I had worked on newspapers. But three months after I returned to civilian life, the Most Reverend Vincent S. Waters, Bishop of Raleigh, North Carolina, asked me if I would come to his diocese to start a Catholic newspaper and serve as executive secretary of the North Carolina Catholic Laymen's Association.

This was not a decision for me alone but for my wife, too. Happily, Barbara was as convinced as I that we should use our talents for the Church. Barbara is a writer, too, and it was her example more than anything else that had led me to study the claims of the Church. So in April, 1946, we decided that for the rest of our lives we'd simply make ourselves available to God and let Him use us as He wished.

Life since that time has been a wonderful adventure. After the newspaper in North Carolina was under way, we left and headed for the University of Notre Dame. There we both studied, and I became director of publications and started the University of Notre Dame Press. After four years there, we returned to North Carolina, opening a Catholic information center on the main street of Charlotte, the least Catholic major city in the nation. It was a financial failure, and yet there were so many opportunities to tell people of Christ and His Church that it was a very rewarding four and a half years we spent there. There were many who knew nothing about the Church when we first met them but who were good Catholics when we left, and we know the center left its mark on the community.

During these years I started to write a letter one day to a local newspaper, protesting the showing of an objectionable film, when I decided that this was not the way to attack the problem. I tore up that letter and wrote one instead to Francis Fink, editor of *Our Sunday Visitor*. I told him I wanted to write a motion picture-television column for his paper. He told me to go ahead and try. The result was that I gained what I honestly believe is the most loyal, most willing-to-serve audience in the world.

It was during the Charlotte years, too, that Archbishop Noll suggested to the National Catholic Welfare Conference that I do the Information Bureau bulletin, a monthly newsletter that reviews the contents of non-Catholic publications for members of the hierarchy and for priests in information center work. I was offered this opportunity, and on starting it I assumed the duties of the director of the Bureau of Information, a position that since has been taken over most capably by Father John Kelly.

In this account of work, I've neglected the most important of all things that happened to us. On the newspaper in North Carolina and in the Catholic information center work, Barbara was my greatest helper, serving along with me. But Barbara and I wanted most of all to have children. After nearly six years of childlessness, we went to St. Anne de Beaupré to ask for children. In the next two years we had two children.

But in the year 1955 we nearly lost our son. A malformed heart made it seem likely, the doctor said, that he would not live to adulthood. It was important that he be kept from colds and infections. The same was true of Barbara, who was given the cross of a serious illness.

We had always hoped we might live for a little while in a foreign country, and after our son Guy's illness we decided that we would go away soon. We chose Spain. But as we made our preparations everything seemed to turn us away from Spain and toward Cuba. When it seemed evident this was what God wanted, we changed our plans to go to Cuba.

We came there knowing no one, but a letter of introduction to Bishop Alberto Martin y Villaverde, Bishop of Matanzas, had preceded us. Four days after we'd arrived we had found a village, San Miguel de los Banos, that we'd never heard of before but that we knew was the village for us the moment we saw it.

Since that time God has used us. Through the readers of *Our Sunday Visitor,* the pastor of the little church in San Miguel has been able to start a Catholic school there and another in Coliseo nearby.

Then the Bishop of Matanzas appointed me to a committee to try to work on ways and means to defend and promote the Faith in the diocese. He said to me, as he explained what was needed, "I believe the Holy Ghost sent you here for just this purpose."

We believe this, too.

This is our life. I have tried to tell of it simply but to show as I told it how God uses those who want to be used.

The world stands in need of lay apostles. Not all, of course, like Barbara and me, are to be writers. There is need for doctors, lawyers, businessmen, laborers, who will say to God that they know that all they are or ever will be comes from Him and so they offer back to Him what He has given them.

It is as simple as that—just making yourself available to God. It may be He will never move you out of your home town, it may be you'll be moved far away, but if you tell God you want Him to use you, then of this I am sure: you will be used.

For those who are married, it must, of course, be a decision made by both husband and wife, for in marriage two are one. For myself, I've never ceased thanking God for Barbara, who made the big difference in my life. She has worked beside me in all I've tried to do.

But for all, it is necessary somewhere along the way to decide what is most important in life. For those who are aware that we are on earth to know, love and serve God and some day gain eternal life with Him in heaven, then this must be what is most important for them.

This doesn't mean that all must start information centers or go to foreign countries. For most their work may be in their home cities in their own jobs. But their aim should be to use their talents to serve Christ and His Church. They must offer themselves to God and let Him have His way.

If they do, then we know it will mean happiness. It won't necessarily mean financial success. It won't mean that God will spare them crosses—sometimes He may well give them even greater crosses. But when they offer themselves to God, even the heaviest cross can be lightened, and trying one's feeble best to do His will is the greatest success possible in this world.

For Happier Families

PAT AND PATTY CROWLEY [1]

I T IS fitting that we write this story of the Christian Family Movement together, for the basis of the movement is husband and wife working as a team to restore the family to Christ. Providentially, our married life has been parallel to and has been involved with its beginnings and growth. Yet, when we settled down after our honeymoon in 1937, our lives were geared to the tempo of the times with their full share of rather meaningless social activities. Still, between the cocktail parties and charity benefits, there was the dream of becoming a living breathing part of the life of the Church—the life of Christ.

Father Charles Sheedy, C.S.C., who was then teaching at Notre Dame, gave substance to the dream by suggesting that we engage in some form of apostolic work. And a few days later when Paul Hazard, an insurance salesman, called to say that he and a companion would like to discuss the formation of a men's Catholic Action group, we were indeed enthusiastic.

[1] Pat and Patty Crowley assisted at the birth of the Christian Family Movement and have contributed immeasurably to its growth and development. In this article they record the fascinating history of this apostolate of the Christian family. Mr. Crowley is a young Chicago lawyer, who devotes much of his spare time to this movement and other apostolic works; Mrs. Crowley also has a full-time job caring for her own four children and many foster children, but she has fully cooperated with her husband in this apostolate.

The Crowleys recently completed a world tour during which they visited many C.F.M. groups in Europe and Asia. The address of C.F.M. headquarters is Room 2010, 100 West Monroe St., Chicago 3, Illinois.

When the group organized it was composed of insurance salesmen, lawyers, teachers, personnel and credit men, with Father Charles Marhoefer as chaplain. Strangely enough, though we all had one thing in common, our married status, it was only after considerable floundering that our point of emphasis became the Christian family: of elevating mere family living, group-living, to sacramental-living, Christ-living. The vagueness of our dream was slowly crystallizing into the vision of consecrating everything in the home to God's service, to be used in His praise and to His greater glory; to make the Christian family truly representative of the Church. This vision might have become lost in the midst of our secular and materialistic environment had it not been heightened by the faith of Msgr. Reynold Hillenbrand, the unflagging work of Father Marhoefer, and our contacts with leading lights in the lay apostolate already reaping a harvest of souls in their particular fields.

We say the faith of Msgr. Hillenbrand because of the staggering impact of his thrilling concept of our part in the Mystical Body. "Christ shares His work with you," he said. "We are the hands of Christ in the most noble sense; where we work, Christ works. We are the feet of Christ in the most noble sense; wherever we go, Christ goes. We are the heart of Christ; wherever we go, the love of Christ is found because we love people. We are the lips of Christ; whatever we articulate, we are articulating for Christ." With such a conviction of our exalted role it is amazing now to ponder the fact that we did become listless, that in the beginning our attendance at meetings was intermittent. Father Marhoefer lifted us from this lethargy by a positive program designed to expand our knowledge of God—how well he knew that such knowledge would inspire love, and the overflow of love must be consumed in action.

We met once a week to study the New Testament and the liturgy, to bring a report on action, and to hold an inquiry— the last being the nucleus of the session where a problem of the environment was subjected to the classic process: see, judge, act. But the meeting was more correctly centered in

Christ. We began to know Him—historically through the pages of the New Testament, contemporaneously as He lives with us, in His Mystical body, renewing His redemption by bringing all things under the sway of His redemptive power. Lay leaders were being formed intellectually, but above all, spiritually. We wanted the world to recognize Christ through the visible reality of genuine Christian lives lived amid circumstances similar to their own. It would be our contribution toward stabilizing a world reeling from internal disorder, dizzy with parental and juvenile delinquency, intoxicated with immorality and untruth. Here the chaplain was indispensable, for we knew that normally God has not decreed that a layman may effectively direct his own or another's spiritual development. Our vision was kept intact, too, by meeting and sharing views with the dedicated laymen whose names read like a galaxy of stars in the glorious firmament of Catholic Action— Catherine and Eddie Doherty, Anne Harrigan of Friendship House, Joanna Danist, who was instrumental in making Childerley Farm a center of inspiration for the laity, Dorothy Day, Carl Bauer at Christ the King Center for men in Herman, Pennsylvania, the Young Christian Workers, the dedicated daughters of Grailville. We lived with them, prayed with them, hoped with them, and were touched by hearing about the heroic dedication of lesser lights whose total consecration will only be fully discerned in the glow of God's perpetual light.

When the men's organization was established, the women organized along similar lines with similar objectives. One of the first significant activities was the women's pre-Cana day for engaged couples, while the men contributed a Cana day for the married—days of recollection for both groups, a project which grew so rapidly that the organization known as the Cana Conference was created to take it over. In retrospect we thrill to recall our first Cana day—the new perspective we gained, the new conception of our participation in the Holy Sacrifice of the Mass. Never again could we remain mere spectators at this divine drama of supreme love.

Yes, the movement was growing. In joy we were reaping

its benefits, living more fully the life of Christ. In thanksgiving we longed to implant everywhere the awareness that the family, the basic unit of society, is one of the chief means through which men are adequately directed toward their supernatural end. We wanted to keep before them the knowledge that when Christ restored the primary indissoluble character of marriage, it was His purpose to provide a permanent pattern of society which was to stand out clearly through the many shifting forms that society might be likely to assume; to spread to the ends of the earth the love that would restore family life in Christ.

It was early apparent that the true significance of the movement would only be realized when it became a couples' effort. To that end, small groups, on a parish level, were formed which providentially became roots from which branches sprang in every direction. Together men and women with equal dignity played their parts according to their nature, distinctive qualities, physical, intellectual, and moral capabilities. Masculine and feminine psychology blended beautifully to great advantage—the men more suited by temperament to deal with public business, external affairs; the women contributing deeper insight for understanding the delicate problems of domestic and family life, and bringing a surer touch to solving them. It was not so much that each sex was called to a different task; the difference was more in a matter of judging and arriving at concrete and practical applications. The strength of the team sank the movement into the solid bedrock of a genuine contribution to society everywhere.

Taking our children with us, we made of our annual vacations opportunities to visit groups of lay workers—learning from them, sharing ideas with them, developing our spiritual life through the Mass and the sacraments, and under the compelling spirituality of superb retreat masters.

Shortly after our first Family Life Conference in Chicago in 1947, our fifth and last child was born—but she was not really the last of our children. In 1948 we were given our first foster child, Algy from Lithuania, who was followed by Margaret, Virginia, Mary Ann, Cathy, Michael and others.

Ultimately they all returned to their parents, but the Catholic Home Bureau insured our always having seven children. In addition, the Exchange Student Program provided us with wonderful daughters—Petra Hermes from Germany, Maria Pinto from Bolivia, Martha Gracias from Rio, Sonia Kucera from Czechoslovakia, Dinh from Viet Nam, Martha and Jane from China. These children were delightful companions for our own, and active, enthusiastic helpers at C.F.M. meetings. As a result of a C.F.M. inquiry on international relations, we invited several foreign students for dinner, and from this beginning we went on to entertain students from Manila, Saigon, Hong Kong, Accra, Tokyo, Formosa, Beirut, Malta, India, and South America—all eager to be shown Christianity in action, all apostolic. As our different worlds touched and merged, we saw how truly men of all nations are God's children, how, irrespective of race, color, or background, all men have the same hopes, the same fears, the same basic quest for God. Universal indeed is the echo of St. Augustine, "Thou hast made us for Thyself, O God, and our hearts are restless till they rest in Thee." Divinely logical indeed is our membership in the Mystical Body.

Our work also brought opportunities for travel which were used to contact actual and potential C.F.M. couples. We delighted to see the movement flourishing in California, and the ideal Christian family life exemplified at the home of our friends Dan and Rose Lucey in Los Angeles. In San Francisco we met and talked with zealous priests and eager seminarians. In Chicago we were inspired by the people of the Catholic Labor Alliance, the Catholic Interracial Council, the Y.C.W., the Young Christian Students, and most of all by our dear friend, Tom Crowe, who lives in our memory as a shining example of Christ-likeness.

In 1948, then acting as president couple of the Chicago Federation of C.F.M., we were encouraged to publish a manual on the formation of a group. As a result, "For Happier Families" was prepared by tired, struggling, but enthusiastic men eager to extend the ideas and the ideals which had so thrilled them. The first edition was launched in June, 1949,

and distributed at the first C.F.M. convention at Childerley
Farm, Illinois. It was at this convention that the couples agreed
to call their organization the Christian Family Movement, and
adopted the paper *Act* as its official publication. Another convention was held in 1950, and one has been held yearly since
then. By 1956, Notre Dame University, where that year's convention was held, opened its doors to welcome 6,000 delegates.

Our extension work grew rapidly, and our lives became
hectic. We attended to our business in the daytime, met
couples in the evening, handled correspondence. Our Chicago
law office was designated as the Chicago headquarters address,
but the real work was done at home. "For Happier Families,"
as revised by Peter and Alma Fitzpatrick, went into five edi-
tions distributed all over the free world, and *Act* continued to
grow from the few hundred circulated in 1946 to the present
18,000 copies distributed monthly.

This progress was made despite the many difficult decisions
and discussions regarding method, policy, and purpose. Haste
was unheard-of, and all shades of opinion were taken into
consideration, for the movement stands for the right of the
individual to express himself. For example, there were arguments for and against the movement's embracing people of all
types of educational, occupational, financial, cultural, and
social background. The result: everyone is welcome. We used
to argue as to whether it was a family movement concerned
only with our homes or a broad movement concerned with all
aspects of family life. Of course the latter belief has prevailed.
The problems presented by a uniform program were discussed,
but with slight adaptation our program has worked well in
East Africa, India, Canada, and many other parts of the world.
In 1952, Peter, then a Japanese visitor to the United States,
despite the gulf of difference in culture, background, history,
and economic conditions, set out to establish the C.F.M. in
Tokyo. It flourished. Recently we saw the little groups in
Tokyo attacking their problems of baby-sitters, money, hous-
ing. We saw in them the same yearning to become individually
Christ-like, and to extend the charity of Christ to their
neighbor.

And so it was everywhere on our recent trip around the world. Everywhere we met a vital enthusiasm for a practical approach to the family apostolate; we saw our fellow-men intent on the educational and prayerful process which reveals to them the mind of Christ Who intended the family to be the handmaid of the Church, a sanctuary of peace, a nursery of virtue and sanctity—an undying flame in the darkness of the world.

A NOTE ON THE TYPE

IN WHICH THIS BOOK WAS SET

This book has been set in Granjon, a lovely Linotype face, designed by George W. Jones, one of England's great printers, to meet his own exacting requirements for fine book and publication work. Like most useful types, Granjon is neither wholly new nor wholly old. It is not a copy of a classic face nor an original creation, but rather something between the two —drawing its basic design from classic Garamond sources, but never hesitating to deviate from the model where four centuries of type-cutting experience indicate an improvement or where modern methods of punch-cutting make possible a refinement far beyond the skill of the originator. This book was composed and printed by The York Composition Company, Inc., of York, Pa., and bound by Moore and Company of Baltimore. The design and typography are by Howard N. King.